ACTA UNIVERSITATIS STOCKHOLMIENSIS

STOCKHOLM STUDIES IN HUMAN GEOGRAPHY

1

EDUCATION AND SOCIETY

The geographer's view

By

TORVALD GERGER and GÖRAN HOPPE

ALMQVIST & WIKSELL INTERNATIONAL

STOCKHOLM · SWEDEN

About the authors

Torvald Gerger (born 1938) is a Senior Lecturer at the Department of Human Geography, the University of Stockholm. He received his Ph.D. in 1968 for a dissertation on migration studies. His research interests nowadays include the geography of education; Swedish modernization and urbanization as well as the project Man, Landscape and Society: An information system for which he is the leader.

Göran Hoppe (born 1946) is a Research Fellow at the Stockholm Human Geography Department. He received his Ph.D. in 1978 and is presently involved in developing the Man, Landscape and Society Information System as well as doing research on the Swedish 19th century enclosure consequences and Swedish industrialization processes. He also continues the educational and literacy research.

Printed in Sweden by
Sundt Offset AB, Stockholm, 1980

Preface

When the decision of the Swedish parliament in 1842 to introduce a compulsory primary school became known, a number of farmers in Locknevi parish expressed their opinion at a parish meeting in the following way:

"If a postponement can be obtained until the next Parliamentary session, we are almost certain that the School Act will come to nothing, as there are already many parishes which do not concern themselves with any building for this purpose but rely themselves on the fact that this project will not be a permanent one ... Secondly, if all children in the parish between 8 and 15 years of age shall study, who is then to do all the work? Those years are quite the best working years, to train the working people. If those years gone, the love of work is gone too. What will be then? A great misery for the future."

Seen in a short time perspective, this negative attitude to the innovation introduced from above by the authorities influenced the every day primary school strongly. In a longer perspective though — and with the results available — we know today that the introduction of the compulsory primary school was an important link in the chain of educational reforms to follow.

That the Locknevi freeholders' words did not come true, has brought about the pleasant fact that we have been able to study the educational development of Sweden for a number of years. We have had the ambition to — principally from an individual perspective — describe both the growth and the consequences. From the title of this book, we are obviously keen to introduce ourselves as geographers, a definition of positions that largely explains the disposition of the studies.

In this preface, we want to testify that the years with the School have been enjoyable. A big part of this joy is due to Brita Hellichius who has helped with data collection, card punching and map drawing. Stefan Fogelvik and Hans Hertling have helped us with computer programs. Hopefully, Wendy Duncan has made our English readable. Many others, both Locknevians and others, have helped in lots of ways — we thank you all.

The main parts of the research work has been financed by the Bank of Sweden Tercentenary Foundation as well as the publication of this book which in turn sums up a number of papers, reports and books published at the Department of Human Geography, the University of Stockholm.

Stockholm april 1980

Torvald Gerger   *Göran Hoppe*

Contents

I. THE SPATIAL STRUCTURE OF SOCIETY
— SOME DEFINITIONS

The arena of man is the cultural landscape and individuals carry out different activities within this landscape. In terms of different time perspectives, there are different sets of relationships between man and the landscape. Man, the landscape and their interdependence together comprise the spatial structure of society.

A society consists of many different elements. The smallest and also the most basic elements of a society and its spatial structure are *individuals* and *livelihood positions.* The actions of an individual on this basic level, which is not influenced by society, are affected mainly by three factor complexes. The first is the individual time-budget — an individual cannot sail to another continent in one day or spend a lifetime reading the daily paper. The time-budget, or the amount of time available to an individual, is thus primarily a question of time-perspective. In one day you can go to work, do some errands, watch television etc. From the view-point of a lifetime, only the major breaks in an individual's life-path which result from certain major decisions can be distinguished.

The second factor affecting the activities of an individual is his spatial position. Depending on the time-perspective taken, spatial position can be seen as either a constraint or a resource influencing the decisions that an individual makes. For example, different forms of labour organization and land-use occur in places which are either near to, or far away from, the central point of a region.

The third factor of influence on the individual level is genetic resources — early intelligence, working capacity etc.

Clearly, many other factors influence individual actions. Such factors are normally related to society and different *groups* of individuals and we shall discuss these in more detail later. Firstly, however, we should examine the other basic element in a society's spatial structure; livelihood positions.

A livelihood position is defined here as the *spatial* position from where an individual can reach the facilities he or she needs for survival. Implicit in this definition is the fact that different livelihood positions are connected with different amounts of recources, from mere survival to immense wealth. and that the amount of resources available can change over time. During a specific period of time, a year or a century, livelihood positions can be moved, created or can disappear as a result of societal or individual actions. In times of population pressure, when the number of livelihood positions in an area may become insufficient, individuals may be forced to leave the area. Individual access to a livelihood positions depends upon factors related to society and different groups in society.

Some of the relationships between different elements of the spatial structure of society are illustrated in Diagram 1. In the first image, people are carrying out different activities. The way they do this depends upon the opportunities offered and limitations imposed by individuals, livelihood positions, formal and informal groups and organizations and relations between groups and organizations. In Sweden, we can include among

8

formal organizations the well-developed school system and the complex labour organizations, as well as different governmental bodies. *Informal* groups consist of the family and other social associations. The relationships between individuals and groups form a specific pattern illustrated here by the second image in Diagram 1.

One example of social restriction and conflicts between different social strata is the way in which resources are transferred from one generation to the next. We can divide societies and areas into different groups according to the form of resource transfer taking place between generations. One extreme is direct and complete transfer where the son or daughter takes over the parent's livelihood position and its associated productive resources. Social mobility does not occur in such societies and the social structure is thus static. It is highly probable that societies of this type are also spatially static as the livelihood positions bind individuals to a specific *place*. If individuals leave permanently, they will also lose their means of survival.

Changes in such a system of resource transfer originate, for example, from conflicts between landed and landless strata — groups which inherit livelihood positions and groups which do not.

The other extreme, in terms of mechanisms of resource transfer, is a society in which only genetic resources are transferred, i.e. only those individual factors outlined above. In such a society, children do not take over their parent's positions and the social structure is completely open. The spatial structure of a society of this extreme character tends to be very flexible as individuals are not bound to specific livelihood positions.

In reality all types of societies, both capitalistic and socialistic, represent forms intermediary between these two extremes. Development, caused by conflicts or other factors of change, may be oriented towards one extreme at one time and towards the other extreme at another. In a country which from the outside appears to have a uniform resource transfer system, there may actually be quite large differences between different places and between town and country.

It is not only the relationships between people, groups and organizations that regulate the way in which different actions are performed. The spatial sub-division of the landscape in terms of different types of exploitation, land use, and form of ownership makes up a pattern of relationships illustrated in image 4 of Diagram 1. Over time, these relationships between individuals and groups, between the landscape and organizations, have formed the cultural landscape we know today. The cultural landscape can thus be said to express the spatial structure of society and its development over time (see image 3, Diagram 1).

Before the coming of man different types of factors influenced the natural landscape. Certain features of the natural landscape impose *restrictions* upon the spatial structure of society which are difficult to change and are therefore normally regarded as given. These include topographical or geological characteristics, and are sketched in image 5 of Diagram 1.

1. People

2. Relationships between people

3. The cultural landscape.

4. Relationships between people and the land

5. The natural landscape

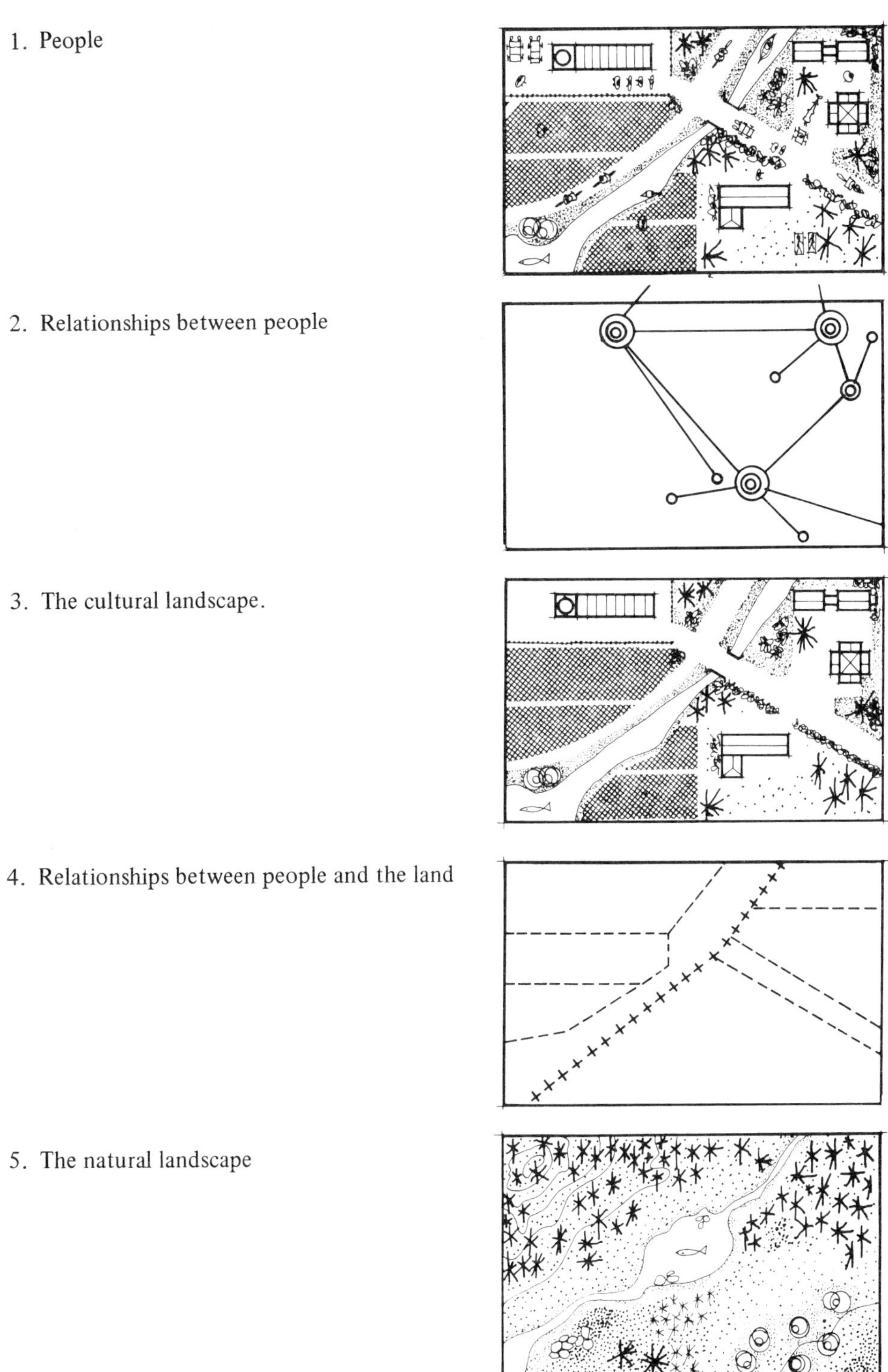

Diagram 1. The spatial structure of society: main concepts.

10

II. SWEDISH DEVELOPMENT
IN A SOCIAL AND SPATIAL CONTEXT

It is possible to distinguish certain major trends in the development of the spatial structure of Sweden over the last 300 years. In this chapter, we shall relate these trends to the elements of the spatial structure of a society which were outlined in the preceding chapter.

If we start with the basic elements — individuals and livelihood positions — it is clear that the major development has been on the space-time level rather than the genetic. Many new livelihood positions have been created during these three centuries, many have disappeared, and many have been replaced by others. The locations of livelihood positions have also shifted — until 1850 almost all new positions were in the countryside and were agrarian in character; since 1850 the majority of new positions have been created in urban areas and have thus been non-agrarian. After 1850 a large number of agrarian positions which had been only recently created, disappeared: in 1850, 90 per cent of the population was agrarian, while today only 5–10 per cent is. The absolute number of livelihood positions has risen from about 1.5 million in the late 17th century to about 8 million today. The reason for this large expansion is probably twofold. Firstly the number of individuals — the population — began to increase rapidly from around 1700 until 1920 in some areas, until 1870 in others. This expanding population needed suitable livelihood positions and in many cases succeeded in creating them. Such positions were largely agrarian. The second reason for the expansion of livelihood positions was the industrial revolution and the type of development which this gave rise to. Industries which were increasing their production constantly needed manual labour and, as most of the important industries were urban-based, a shift in the location of livelihood positions occurred, causing a population flow from rural to urban areas.

One condition for this industrial expansion was an increasing population. As has already been mentioned, the population increase began at least a century before the industrial transition in Sweden. Much has been written on this subject and on the relationship between technical innovations and population expansion but there is no clear-cut, convincing explanation of *why* the population started growing. Two main schools of thought on this matter can be identified. The oldest, and until recently the most dominant, is the Malthus school, based upon the thoughts of Malthus (see Malthus 1872). This school sees technical (for example agrarian and medical) innovations as being the main cause of population growth — population space expands and, consequently, the population starts growing (see Habakkuk 1971). For some reason the "checks" on population growth outlined by Malthus do not operate. In the 1960's, a new school of thought inspired mainly by the Danish economist Ester Boserup (see Boserup 1965) became popular. Boserup sees population growth as an independent factor in relation to technical development — when a population starts growing, innovations and the use of new techniques are stimulated by the pressure on available resources. A sort of intermediary idea concerning the relationship between population growth and technical development has been proposed by Grigg (see Grigg 1976).

Population development has been quite different over space and time and both schools of thought would probably be able to gain support for their hypotheses in different *areas* and on different *levels* of a society's spatial structure. In the next chapter, which describes the development of a Swedish parish over a period of 300 years, we shall give some examples of explanations of population growth on the local level.

Before this large population expansion, the nature of *resource transfer* in Sweden was closer to the first extreme outlined in chapter one than the second. Mobility between the landed and the landless strata was about the same upwards as downwards, and the social structure was less open than today. If you were born into one social stratum, you usually remained in it all your life. We know relatively little of the *spatial* mobility of individuals before 1750, partly because of the fact that the sources (parish registers, taxation registers etc.) are incomplete and do not necessarily include all social strata or any information on spatial mobility (for an example of 17th century population mobility, see Åkerman 1977). These sources seldom allow measurement of spatial mobility or its extent until the beginning of the great population growth.

During the population growth period, the struggle for survival became more intense than it had been previously. The new livelihood positions generated in the agrarian sector through freehold-splitting and the clearing of arable land provided opportunities for quite a lot of people, but the population growth was so rapid that, after 1800, the numbers of those not owning property (for example crofters, cottagers and paupers) increased rapidly. Early researchers thought that the population growth was due to increased fertility and decreased mortality within the landless stratum but recently a number of microdemographers (for example, Winberg 1975 and Martinius 1977) have found that the fertility increases actually took place within the landed strata. However, the increase in propertied livelihood positions did not keep pace with the increase in fertility, so that many of the freeholders' children were rendered landless. Nevertheless their better initial positions often made them more successful than landless children in the competition for crofters positions, which lay somewhere between the propertied and the non-propertied positions. Hence, the population growth up to 1870–80 resulted in a society with a slightly enlarged landed stratum, which was able to transfer resources to only a part of the next generation. The remainder were proletarianized, thus contributing to the large increase in the number of landless people.

What were the spatial consequences of this population growth? As has been mentioned, the largest growth occurred between 1750 and 1880 and was predominantly agrarian. The new livelihood positions were generally located in rural areas until the onset of the industrial revolution as those people who were proletarianized or were pushed out of their local system were at first forced to try and make a living in the countryside. With the beginning of industrialization, around 1850, new positions appeared in towns. A growing stream of people moved to the expanding urban areas; at the same time (beginning around 1850) there was a large-scale migration of people to North America. In chapters V, VII and VIII we shall try to explain why some people emigrated and others not in terms of their educational background.

The *relationships* between individuals, and between formal and informal organizations have also undergone major changes. Firstly, the local society in the old sense could be said to embrace the village or, at the very most, the parish. Today, very few of the activities of formal and informal organizations take place on this level. The communal reforms which began in the 19th century and continued until 1974 increased the size of local areas so that, today, the smallest administrative unit is much larger than the old parish. This is the smallest area for which any formal organization can plan its activities.

We can give some examples: village schools have completely disappeared, to be re-

12

placed by large schools situated far apart; labour organizations have amalgamated their local districts into larger units; and farmer and consumer cooperatives have become highly centralized compared with the situation some decades ago. A proposal to expand the size of the counties is being discussed at the moment as the present counties are considered too small to function as administrative units on the regional level. The extent of individual influence on formal organizations has undergone a transition too. When communes and school boards, for example, were amalgamated, much of the opportunity for individual influence disappeared. Fewer individuals are represented in the planning process and in over-seeing activities — whereas previously maybe ten to twenty local parish councils with 100–200 persons were involved in this, today perhaps only 20–30 council members direct the activities of anyone commune.

The consequences of this centralization process for individuals have been largely spatial. To get to school a child may now have to travel ten to twenty miles, whereas in earlier days the village school was just around the corner. If a house-holder wants to go shopping at the local cooperative, the situation is the same. When formal organizations are centralized, people also tend to move to "central" places so as to optimize their time budgets.

Industry has also undergone a centralized trend since the time of the industrial transition. In the beginning, small sawmills, ironworks and so on dominated the picture — today all ironworks in Sweden are under the same management and are located in only half a dozen places. People have little choice but to follow livelihood positions; hence, a strong tendency towards urbanization is induced by industrial centralization.

What about the so-called informal organizations? As the multigenerational 'extended' family has proven to be a largely fictional construct, we can say that no significant transition in family structure has taken place in Sweden during the last 300 years. However, families do usually consist of fewer children now because of the declining birthrate and these children often stay at home for 20 years or more.

The structure of social groups has undergone major changes however. In the agrarian society, and in the early industrial sites, people lived and worked in almost the same place and formed a closely interwoven group, both spatially and socially. Of course, there were different social strata in an agrarian village; the crofters, the cottagers and the farmhands formed one stratum, the freeholders another, etc. and conflicts between these social groups were probably common. But inside one stratum there was a sort of community — a family community and a working community — that has largely disappeared today. One reason for this is the division between the place of work and the place of residence; they are seldom located in the same place, and the family community is not the same as the working community.

The social classes of the 17th century — the classes of the Lutheran social order prescribed in the "hustavla" (see Pleijel 1970) — have gradually been transformed. During the period of population growth, the lower classes expanded extremely rapidly but, after 1900, no great proletarianization took place. It is, of course, very difficult to define a social class or group but an equalizing trend on the national level is evident in some respects — the real income attained by the medium and lower strata is more equal today, for example. At the same time, however, a new trend towards the creation of a landed-landless division has emerged, particularly in cities. If we look at the equalization of opportunities on a regional or local level, we find instead a more accentuated *spatial* inequality forming as a consequence of centralization. This is certainly not unique to Sweden and may perhaps be unavoidable in a modernization process of the kind through which Sweden has passed.

In the previous chapter, the inter-relationships between the landscape, the people and formal organizations were discussed. In some areas of Sweden, urbanization and industrialization implied a changing and intensified land-use, often on former agrarian land of great value (see Helmfrid 1978 and Lewan 1974). In other areas, usually less central in terms of spatial structure on the national level, land-use became less intensive.

This implies that some quite obvious spatial conflicts influenced the direction of development. On the one hand, falling relative market prices for agricultural products and the desire for a higher standard of living forced farmers to rationalize and intensify their activities and to enlarge their farms. On the other hand, proletarianized people exerted strong pressure in favour of freehold-splitting and land reform during the 18th and 19th centuries in conflict with for example the aims behind the enclosure reforms of the 19th century (see Helmfrid 1961). The conflict was probably less intense where the rationalization and mechanization processes were restricted by the natural landscape or by complicated ownership patterns. During the 20th century, the main forces operating against agrarian rationalization in central areas have been the land needs of the production industry and the building of urban residences. In the periphery, the lack of raw materials for the forest industry has led to pressure on farming land. As forests require less intensive land-use than farming the land-use conflict here revolves around "extensification" rather than intensification, as in the rural-urban fringe.

Patterns of ownership and land disposition have certain implications for the spatial structure of society. We have already discussed this to some extent, but a brief description of this development during the period of interest is necessary as a background to the local studies. In the 17th century, there were three major types of land-holdings. The first was the land owned by farmers, freehold land subject to taxation; the second consisted of the estates owned by the nobility, which were free of major taxes; and the third type of holding was the land owned by the king, the government and the Church, which was let to different tenants. The internal spatial structure of these different units was probably not very different in the 17th century, although the units were usually of varying sizes — freehold units were quite small, while the other two types sometimes extended to several parishes. When the population began to increase, opportunities for the proletarianized and the proletariat were quite different on the different types of domains. The power of the nobility and the Church enabled them to keep an almost constant spatial structure with no "secondary" buildings, while the freeholders' villages and domains came to contain the majority of landless people, with the exception of the restricted numbers of tenant farmers, crofters and farmhands tending the nobility and Church holdings (a striking example is given by Nordström (1957)). The sub-division of agrarian units also affected mainly freeholders' domains. Thus the pattern of ownership developed differently for different types of holdings: the freeholders' domains were increasingly sub-divided, while the nobility, government and Church estates were able to retain virtually the same spatial structure.

From the beginning of the 18th century, the differences in legal restrictions and in patterns of taxation between the different types of domains gradually disappeared. All privately-owned land is now subject to taxation and the legal restrictions apply to everybody. The trend towards rationalization in the agrarian sector has resulted in the amalgamation of many of the formerly sub-divided freeholdings into new, larger units adapted to modern techniques. On the other hand, many of the large estates previously owned by the nobility have undergone sub-division, indicating that there has been a movement towards a uniform agrarian unit size.

III. DEVELOPMENT ON THE LOCAL LEVEL:
LOCKNEVI PARISH 1680–1980

A. The Locknevians: Generally gay and happy, also calm and peaceable when left alone, buth otherwise fiery, hard-working, civil and complainant. Pretty women, mostly.

(Anders Ekbaeck 1828)

B. The Development in the Area

Locknevi parish is located in the diocese of Linköping and in the county of Kalmar, about 15 miles from Vimmerby (see Map 1). The parish today consists of 50 ”jordregisterenheter” (taxation register units) and in them a number of small villages or hamlets. Nowadays there are few people living in the parish, just over 570, but in the mid-18th century the population was over 2700. Since the mid-1600's, the main industries have been farming and forestry.

The parish imposes natural restrictions upon the agrarian industry of a somewhat remarkable kind. Only in the central valley running from north to south are there fields of any fertility — the place-names ending in -inge, -stad and -vi, all of a prehistoric character, are evidence of very early settlements here. The rest of the parish is largely located above the highest coastline and has meagre and stony soil. *The natural landscape* has thus been a real obstacle to the development of the main industries.

During the 17th century, there were five estates in Locknevi.[1] Along with the property owned by the Church, they were all located in the central and rather fertile valley (which were consequently dominated by the upper classes) while the freeholders and tenant farmers generally had to be content with less fertile soil in the periphery of the parish (see Map 2). Crofts were established on the estates and their corresponding tenant farms during the 17th and 18th centuries (see Elgeskog 1945). Crofters were contracted to work certain days at the estate (corvée duties) and this work usually dominated their working time (see Hägerstrand 1946). Many crofts had good development potential and, during the 18th century, the estates transformed several into tenant farmers, of which quite a number were sold. To replace these, the number of crofts inside the remaining domain was increased. The estate-owner of Toverum and Lidhem also started a small iron-works in the south-western part of the parish around 1750 to increase his income. This gave not only smiths and their assistants the chance to earn a living, but bog-ore and charcoal also had to be produced and delivered from far away. Croftnames such as "Koltorpet" (The Charcoal Croft) on the estate of Locknevi still remind us of the activities that took place there.

During the 18th century secondary settlements greatly increased in number in line with a rapid population growth, and crofts on freehold land began to appear. In earlier days, almost all settlements had been located in the hamlets; one reason for this was probably the small population (around 500 in 1700) and another the legal restrictions upon croft-establishment on freeholders' domains. The size of the cultivated area and meadow greatly increased in the 18th century, and continued to expand until the first decades of the 20th century. The peak was reached around 1910. During the 18th century many of the freeholders' domains were also sub-divided, often many times over, so that farms became progressively smaller.

The 19th century was largely a continuation of the development of the 18th. The sub-division of freehold land decreased in extent as a consequence of legal measures and restrictions (in cases where farmers had too many children, many were directed to crofts and cottages, or encouraged to emigrate), while the number of secondary settlements continued to increase, predominantly on the freeholders' domains. After 1870, the total population began to decrease, although changes between different social strata took place. Many tiny settlements (crofts, cottages etc.) were sold when the legal restrictions against freehold sub-division were lifted in the late 19th century. Often they were inhabited for only a short time for, as Sweden became industrialized, Locknevi was left hopelessly behind and the number of acceptable livelihood positions diminished. One reason for this was the closing of the Toverum ironworks because of international competition in the 1880s.

---

[1] For a discussion of the Swedish landholding structure, see Appendix 4.

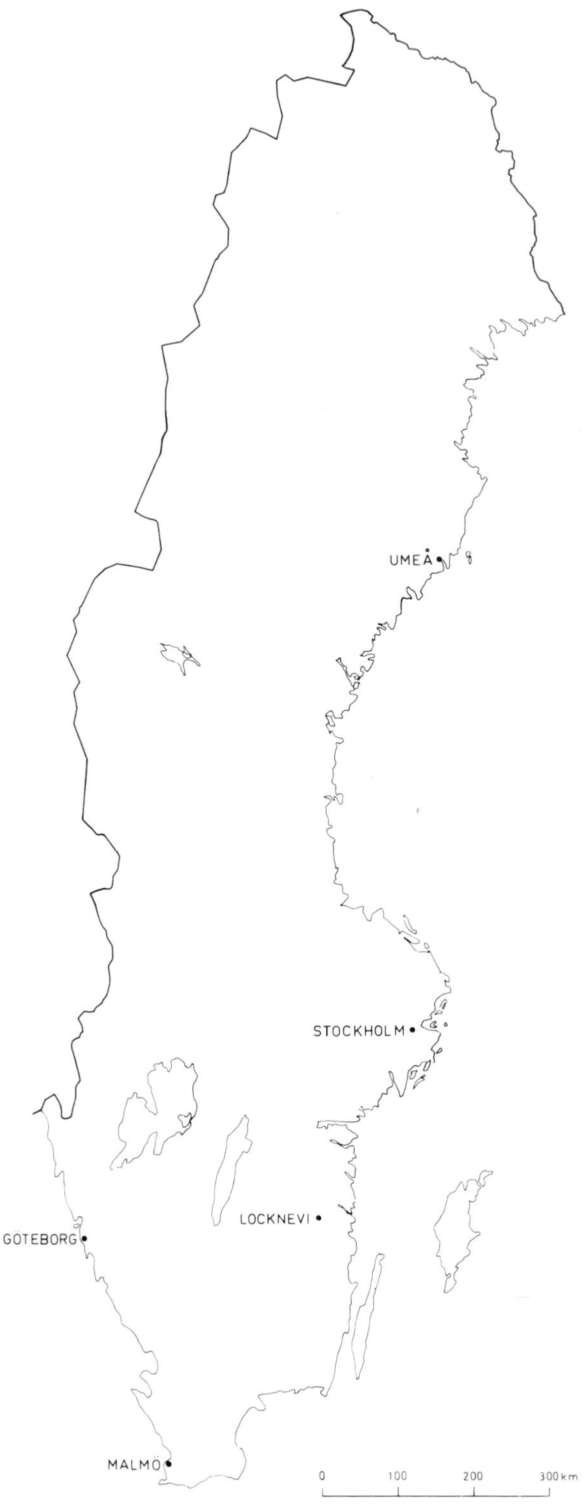

Map 1. Locknevi's spatial location in Sweden.

Map. 2. The spatial structure of Locknevi parish.
Underlined place-names correspond to old estates.

18

By the 1850s, emigration from Locknevi was already taking place on a large scale: during the peak years of 1868 and 1869 more than 100 persons moved to North America. The composition of the emigration flow will be discussed later; here we only want to establish the fact that 19th century Locknevi could not accommodate all its inhabitants at a level judged to acceptable — those who were able to moved, others were forced into a life of the outmost destitution, often starvation.

With the beginning of industrialization, outside Locknevi, new opportunities to improve their standard of living were suddenly made available to the less well-off. Migration from the parish increased as people's expectations were raised. The restrictions imposed on Locknevi in terms of the physical landscape as well as the cultural meant that only a few positions of a "modern" standard were possible to create.

In order to paint a more concrete picture of the development process, we shall now examine the development of three different areas in Locknevi over a period of three hundred years. The first we shall take a look at is the Locknevi estate; the second is Grönhult's little hamlet; and the third is Vrångfall's village (see Map 3).

In 1703, the estate of Locknevi consisted of around 130 acres of cultivated fields and 500 acres of meadow. The inhabitants of the domain probably numbered around a hundred, mainly crofters and their families and a few agricultural workers managing the main unit — the mansion and its immediate surroundings. During the 18th century, eight of the former twentyone crofts were sold off in times of personal economic crisis. Without these crofts, by 1806 the remaining estate consisted of 60 acres of cultivated land and 425 acres of meadow (see Map 4). The cultivated area was enlarged continuously during the 19th and 20 centuries — mainly through the hard labour of generations of crofters. In Maps 5—6 we can see how this clearing took place.

Locknevi Manor House.

In Diagram 2 the settlements of the estate are represented by trajectories illustrating the lifetime and character of each settlement. In Diagrams 3 and 4 we can study population development on the domain; Diagram 3 shows the spatial development and Diagram 4 the social. We can see that the landless strata — C and D — increased while the number of landed remained quite constant over time. This was due *not* to an increase in the number of persons living in each settlement but to the increasing number of settlements (crofts) established. On the central parts of the estate, we can see that the population remained constant while the peripheral parts were cleared for cultivating and living. In the "main unit" — the mansion and its immediate surroundings — the number of landless labourers grew because of the enlargement of the central cultivation area.

Paupers and old people were "taken care of" in several peripheral crofts, probably for a small sum of money paid annually by the parish — this was a common system of poor relief during the 18th and 19th centuries (see Ejdestam 1969). However, it was not very successful, and many of the landless ended their days in starvation and poverty.

The population of Locknevi estate has been gradually decreasing since 1892. The peripheral crofts were deserted first, followed by the more central units. One or two were bought by former crofters during the first half of the 20th century but have also since been deserted. Today, as can be seen from the map, only the smaller parts of the estate are under cultivation and the population numbers less than 40.

Map 3. The location of the areas described.

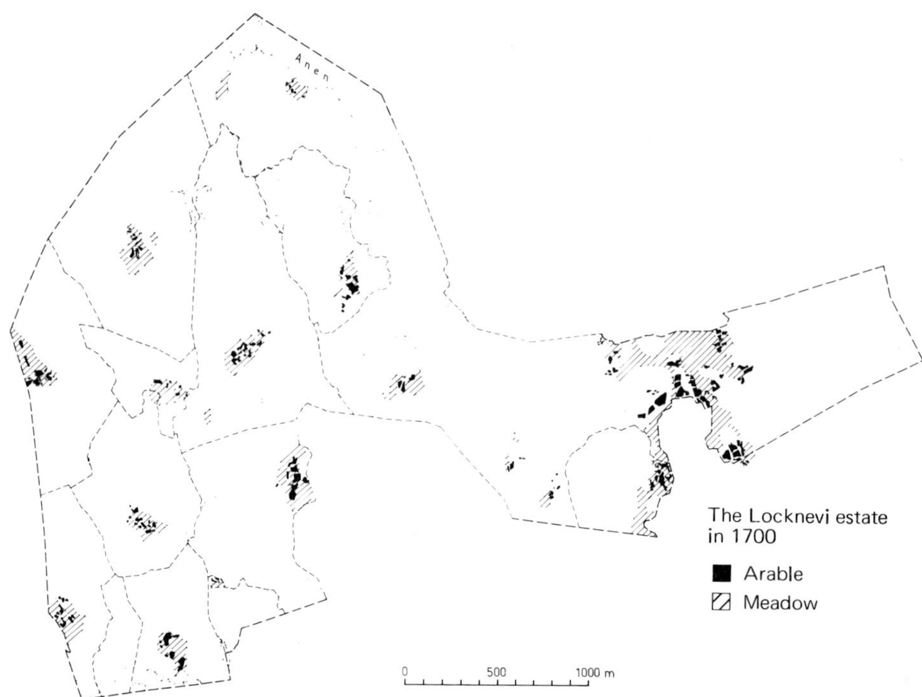

Map 4. The Locknevi estate in 1700.

Map 5. The Locknevi estate in c:a 1800.

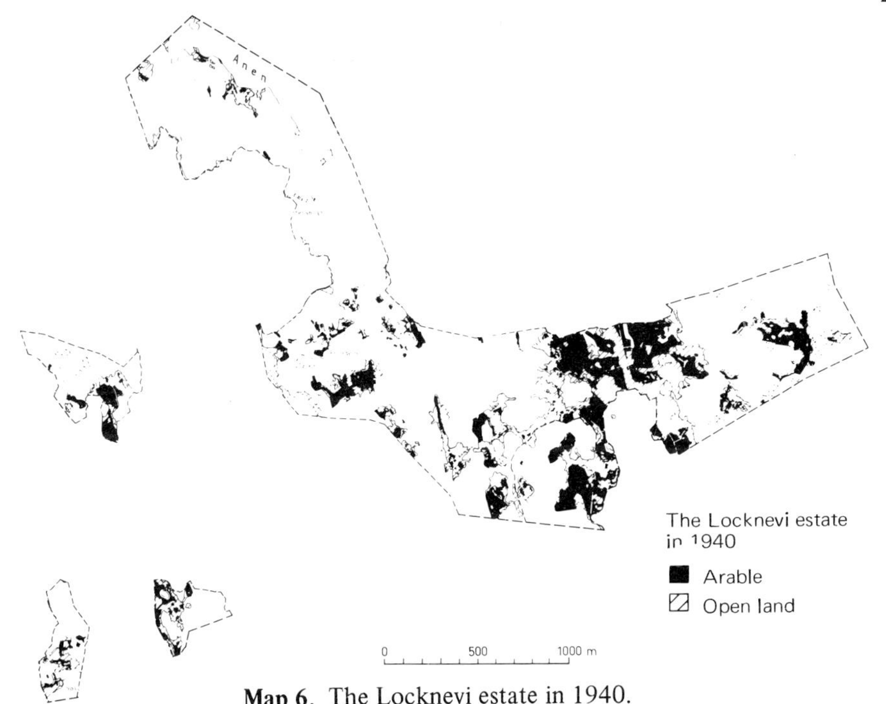

Map 6. The Locknevi estate in 1940.

We shall now pass on to the development of Grönhult. In 1703, there was only one family of crofters living there (probably less than 10 persons) and the size of the cultivated area was perhaps 4 acres. During the 18th century, no less than 8 crofts were established, the population increased to 40, and the area under cultivation was enlarged to a little more than 20 acres. New settlements were established during the first half of the 19th century, and the area under cultivation continued to grow. By around 1850 70 persons lived in Grönhult, but after that the decline began. We should note that not all newcomers could be accomodated despite the intensification and expansion of agriculture — many went abroad or left the area. Thus, the "Boserupian intensification" (see Boserup 1965) was insufficient; as were the "Malthusian population checks" (see Malthus 1872). Today 5 persons live permanently in Grönhult; the initial croft is deserted and only two of the 19th century settlements are inhabited.

Vrångfall in wintertime.

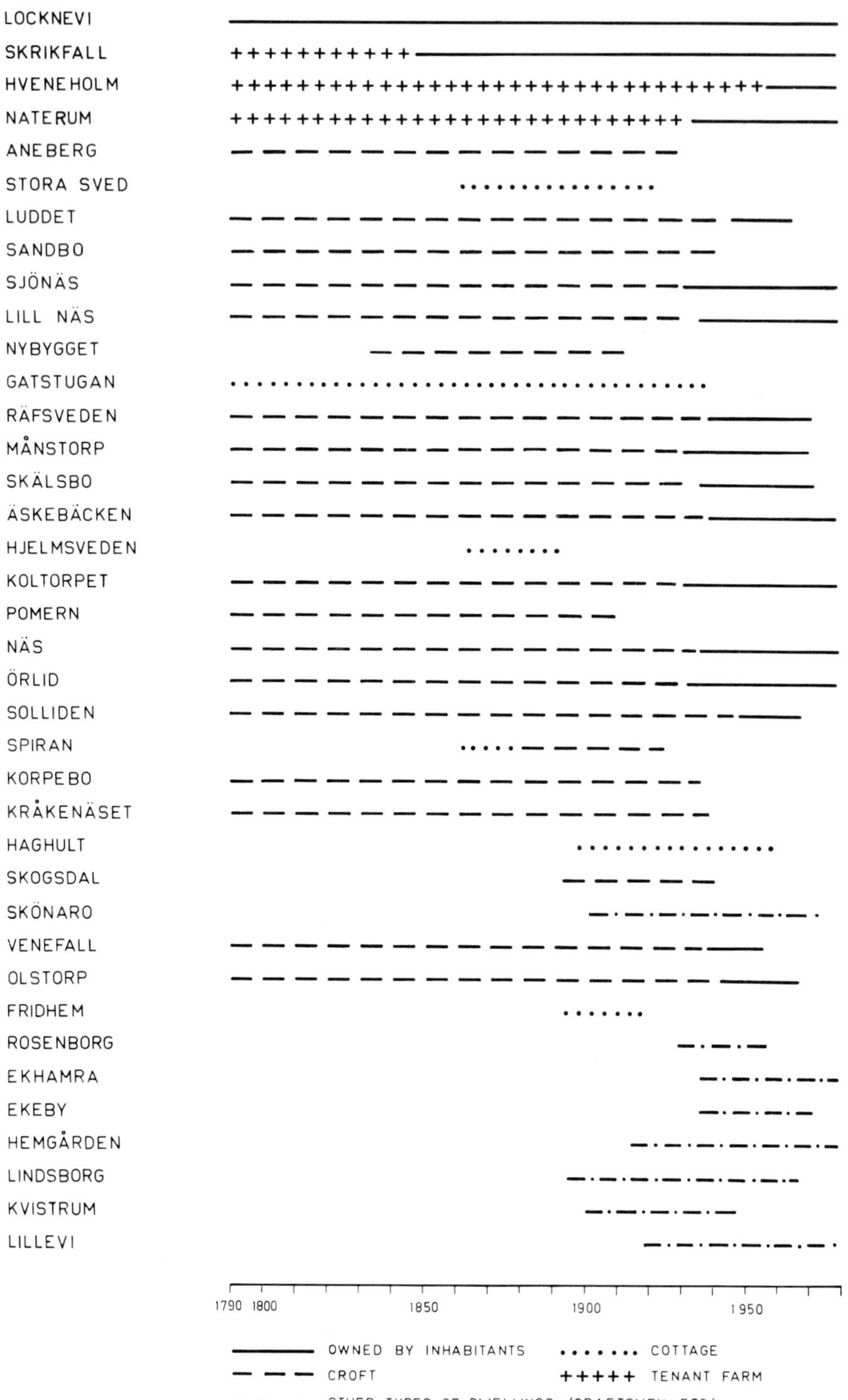

Diagram 2. Lifetime trajectories of the various dwellings in Locknevi estate domains 1790–1980.

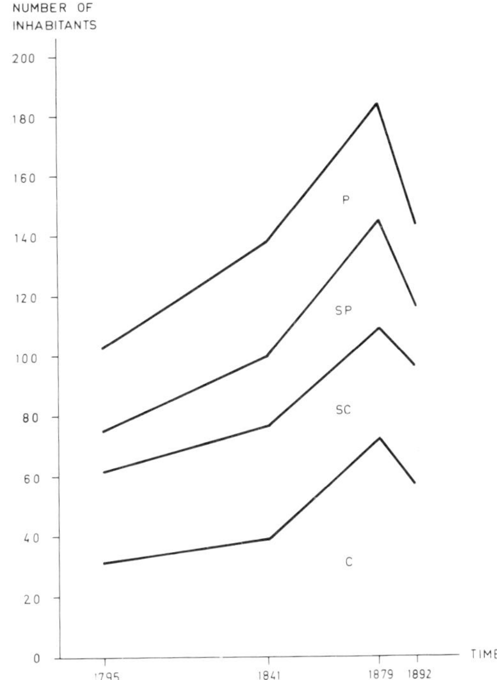

LEGEND:

P = PERIPHERAL DWELLINGS
SP = SEMI-PERIPHERAL DWELLINGS
SC = SEMI-CENTRAL DWELLINGS
C = CENTRAL DWELLINGS

Diagram 3. Population distribution on the Locknevi estate over time: Spatial classification.

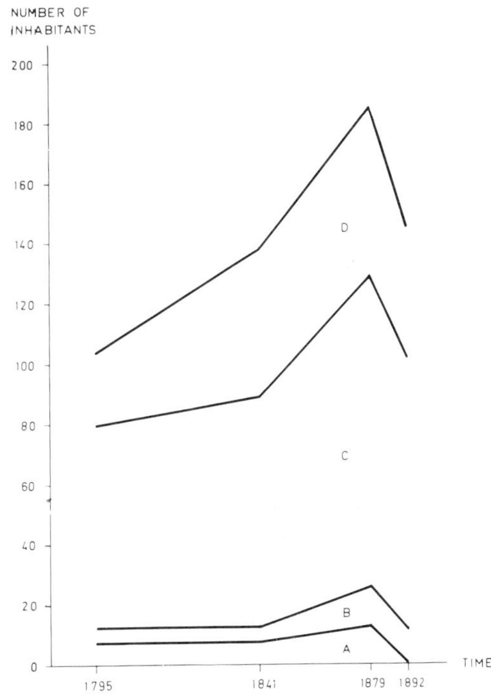

LEGEND:

A = HIGHEST SOCIO-ECONOMIC STRATUM
B, C = INTERMEDIATE STRATA
D = LOWEST SOCIO-ECONOMIC STRATUM

Diagram 4. Population distribution on the Locknevi estate over time: Social classification.

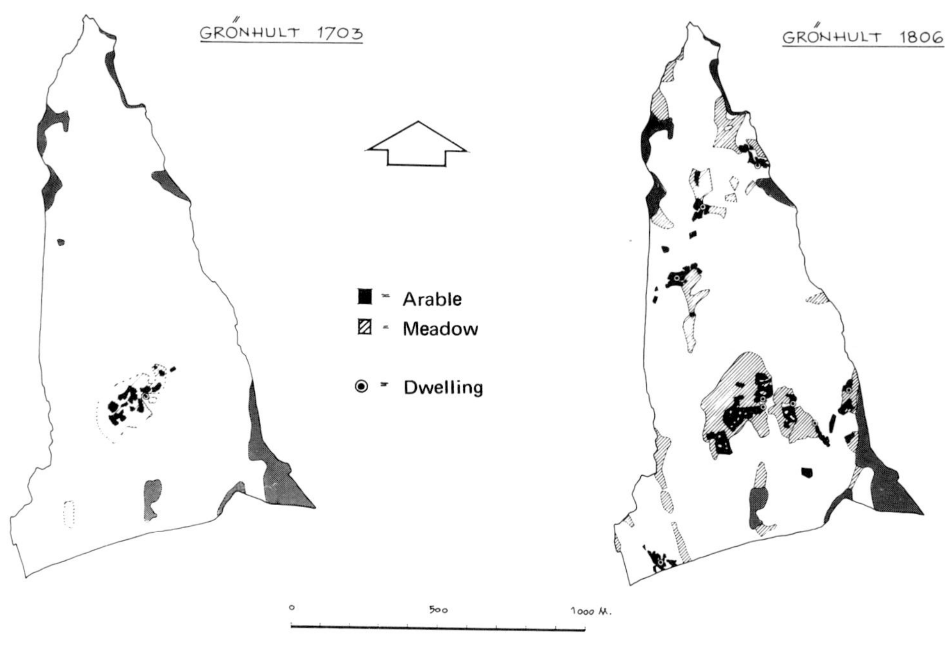

Map 7. The hamlet of Grönhult in 1703 and 1806.

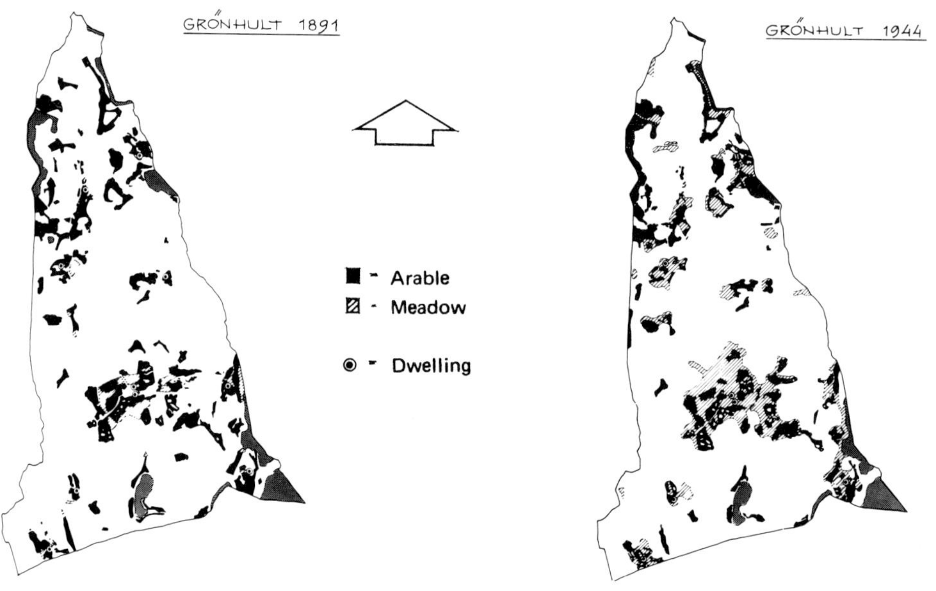

Map 8. The hamlet of Grönhult in 1891 and 1944.

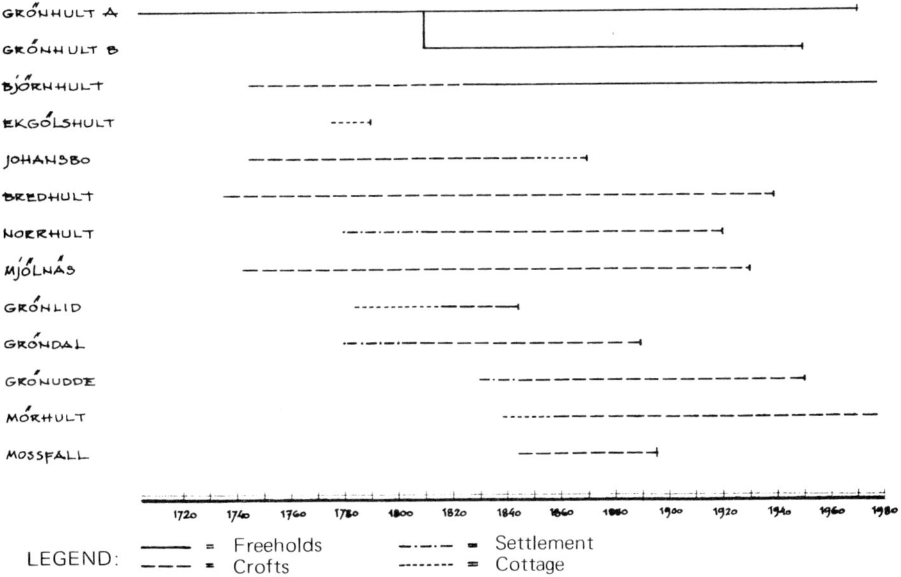

Diagram 5. Life time trajectories of the Grönhult dwellings.

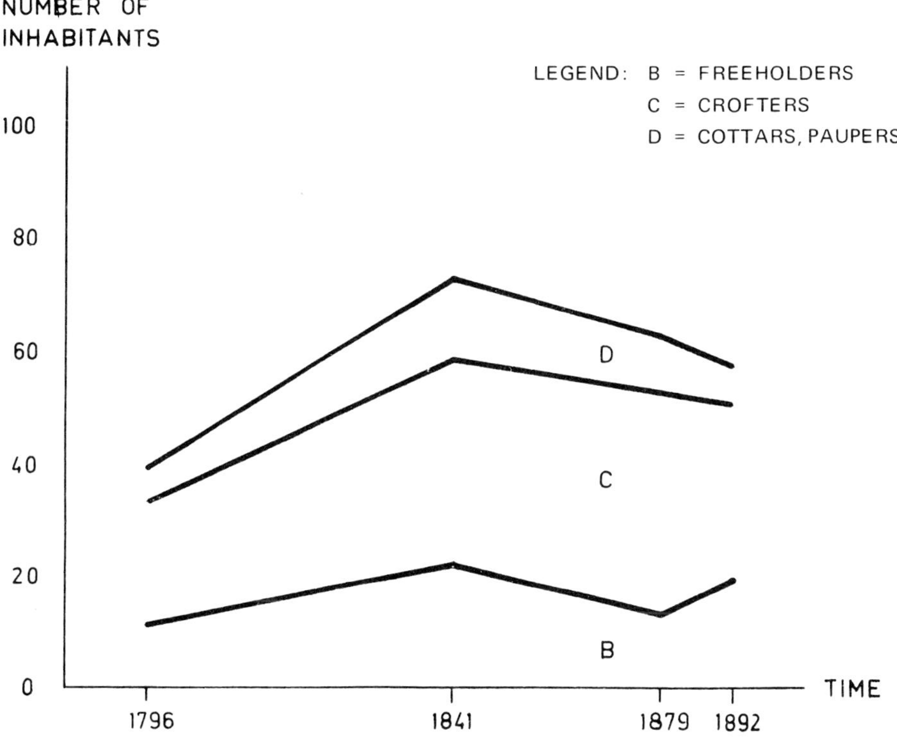

Diagram 6. Population socioeconomic distribution in the hamlet of Grönhult 1896–1892.

Arable of a Vrångfall cottage.

Grönhult arable.

Vrångfall's village, finally (see Maps 9–11), has followed a slightly different line of development. This is not very surprising as the village was due for taxes (see Appendix 4) and thus had a lot of legal duties from which the estates were free. In 1703, there were three farmers and their households in Vrångfall and the area under cultivation was probably limited to around 10 acres. By the end of the 18th century, the number of freehold farms had increased to eight and there was also a grenadiers croft just outside the village (for further information about the old system of military organization, see Kumm 1949). But otherwise, there were no secondary settlements at all, and no landless people except for the grenadier and his household (see Diagram 7–8).

During the 19th century, five small units (crofts, cottages) were established and the population doubled before reaching its peak in 1880. This increase was due mainly to an increase in the number of landless, who again began to decrease in number after 1880. After 1900, the population size stabilized – in part because of the "central" role of the village in the local system of Locknevi parish. A store was opened in 1906, the school-master, the primary school-master and their households were established in the village in the late 19th century and a combined transport and sawmill industry was started. During the last 10 years, however, the population has begun to decrease again; the store has closed, the school had its final term in 1960 and the sawmill has cut down its operations.

If we study the development of the area under cultivation in Vrångfall, we can see that the extent of this area increased markedly between 1795 and 1851; much more, in fact, than the doubling of the population would indicate. In spite of the rapid population growth, some people in Vrångfall (probably landed) did improve their socio-economic positions. After 1851 land continued to be cleared; the peak was reached around 1920.

In the previous chapter, the relationships between technical development and population growth as seen by Malthus and Boserup were outlined. The three village examples given here do not seem to verify either theory. This is due mainly to the fact that both theories were formulated by political economists and probably relate to the national level, although Bosetup does give some local (but rather trivial) developing country examples. For an explanation that holds true on both the regional and local levels, you must also take into account the social structure, the authority structure and the spatial structure, for example. Although the clearing of new land within a certain village area may result in an increase in fertility, the overall population size may not increase at all if the dominant stratum so decides. In the same way, an "independent" population growth may lead merely to the expulsion of large numbers of people from their local systems, irrespective of whether this is a parish or a county. In order to explain societal development, the different levels of the spatial structure of the society must be taken into account and used as a basis for explanatory models.

28

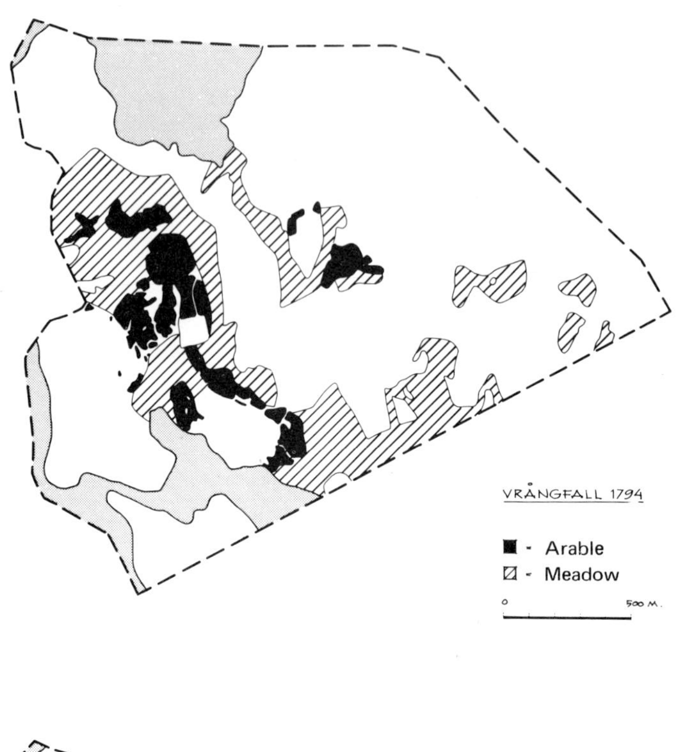

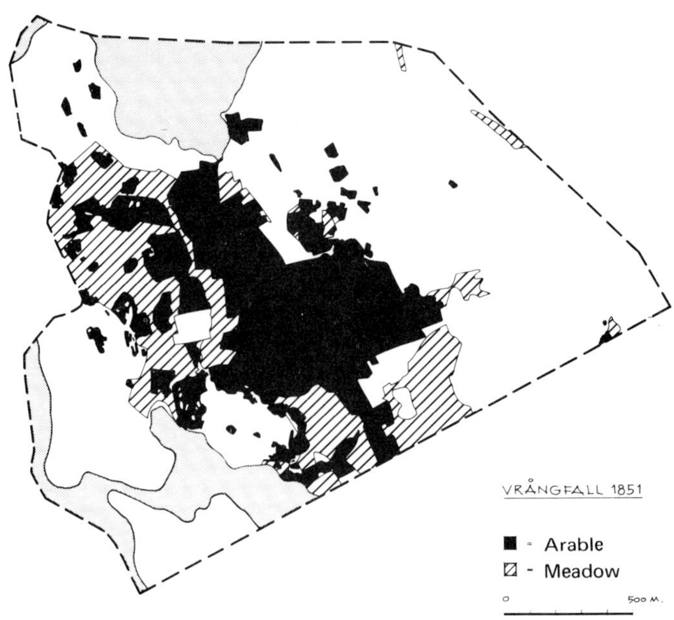

Map 9. Vrångfall village in 1794 and in 1851.

Map 10. Vrångfall village in 1940 and in 1975.

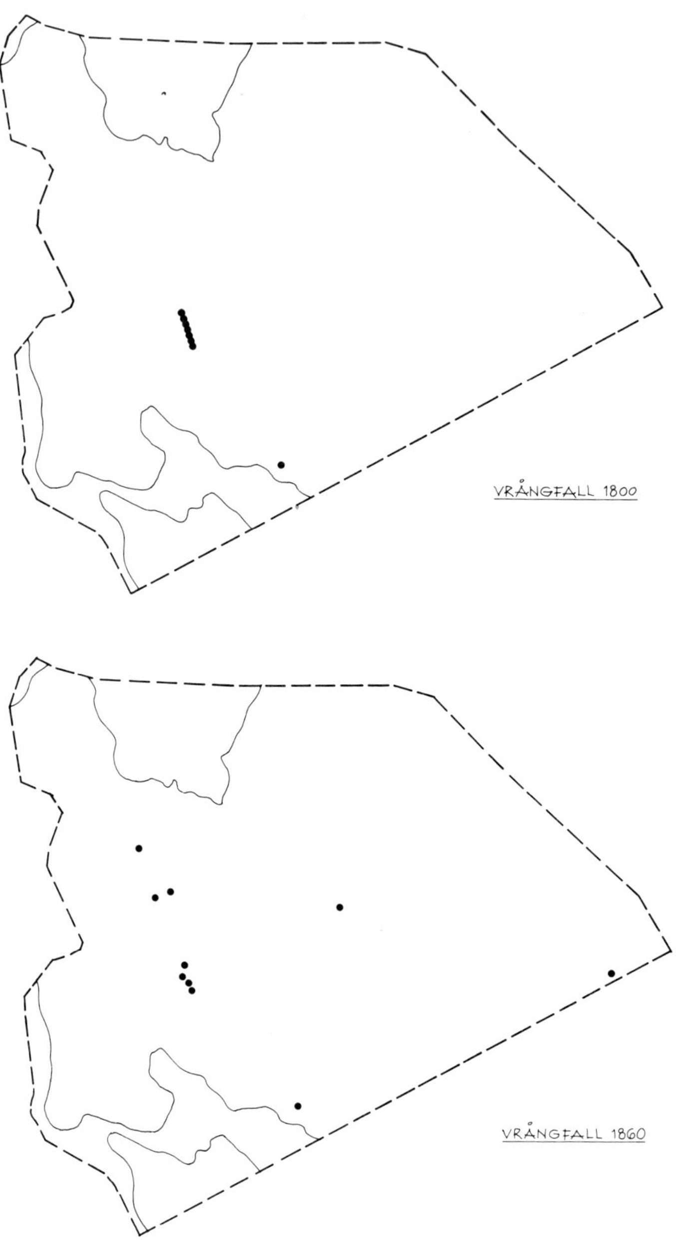

Map 11. The dwellings of Vrångfall 1800–1860.

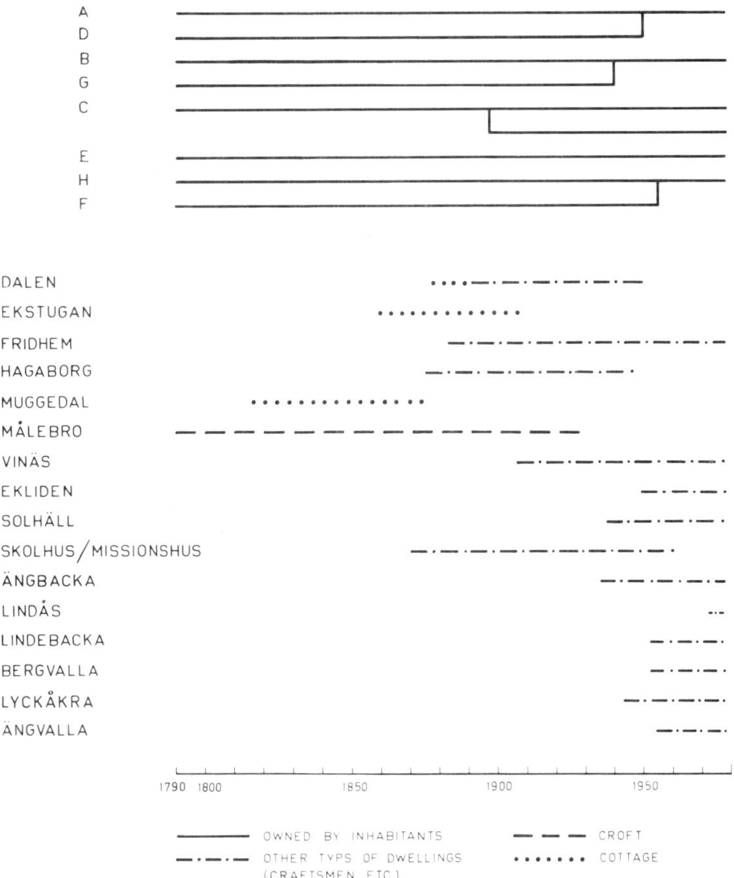

Diagram 7. Lifetime trajectories for the dwellings in Vrångfall village 1790–1980

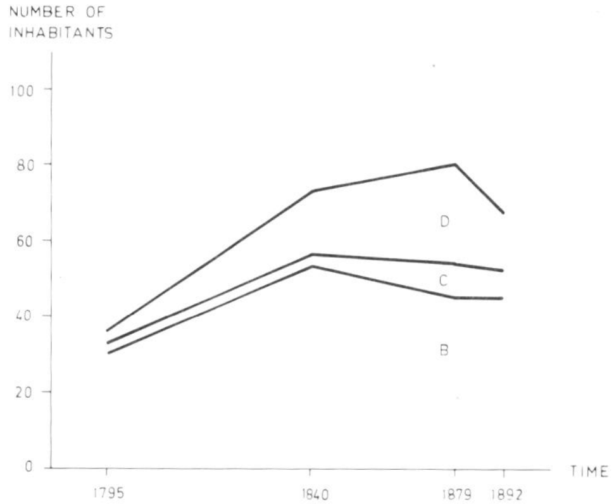

Diagram 8. Distribution of population in social strata. Vrångfall 1795–1895.
For a legend, see Diagram 6.

IV. THE LOCKNEVI PROJECT

The Locknevi Project must be seen against the background presented above concerning society's spatial structure and the processes which change it. The project was begun in 1975 after some feasibility studies had been conducted. At present, the project consists of two major parts:

1.   Education and the Organization and Development of Society.
2.   Man, Landscape and Society: An Information System.

The first part was to be completed in 1979, while the second part runs from 1978 to 1981. A complete bibliography of project reports published prior to 1980 can be found at the end of this book.

Education and the Organization and Development of Society

The aims of this part of the project were to yield more knowledge concerning the estabment and acceptance of the compulsory and the voluntary systems of education in Sweden from around 1850 until the present day. The aim was also to examine the consequences of this development for the individual and for the social and spatial structure of society. The different aims led to three major investigations: one on recruitment to compulsory education and voluntary higher education from 1850 and onwards; and two on the development of individual life-paths for persons born between 1830 and 1880 and between 1928 and 1949. The population studied were all living in Locknevi parish at the age of ten.

Man, Landscape and Society; An Information System

The purpose of this part of the Locknevi Project, as yet unfinished, is to construct an information system which includes important information concerning the spatial structure of society and its changes. The information system will be based on Church Registers, maps, taxation registers, interviews, fieldwork and so on, and will consist of three separate data bases. As the Demographic Data Base for Locknevi, which forms Data Base A (see below), covers the time from 1820 until 1899, the information system will initially cover this period.

A data base is made of *objects* (for example people, real estate, places of work) and their *qualities* (to be born on a certain day, to be located at certain coordinates, to produce milk). The Locknevi information system will include the following three data bases:

Data Base A
Object: PEOPLE

Qualities: demographic

date of birth
date of death
parish of birth
sex
civil status
position in the family (father, mother,
    child)
status in the family (relation to parents,
    children, husband/wife)
mobility

Qualities: occupation

profession
location of place of work

Qualities: dwelling

location of the dwelling *situation:*

a.   on a certain property
b.   at certain coordinates

Data Base B
Object: REAL ESTATE

Qualities: physical structure

area
bed-rock quality
quaternary deposits
topography
land use (field, meadow, structure, forest,
    water, house site . . .)
buildings: location
buildings: use

Qualities: form of organization

owner
tenant
real estate designation

Data Base C
Object: PLACE OF WORK

Qualities:

designation
situated on a certain property
type of production
owner
buildings: location
buildings: use
occupation: number of persons
occupation: profession

The main thrust of the Locknevi Project until 1981 will be to get the information system going. This means that we hope to be able to go through the whole procedure from the processing of incoming data to the output of the products that such a system can offer. In addition, we also intend to test the information system with some specific scientific problems. In brief, they are:

1. Occupational Structure and Location of Work

The development of Swedish society has resulted in the spatial concentration of work. New work opportunities have arisen within industry and services; the agrarian society has disappeared and Sweden has become urbanized. In an historical description of the spatial structure of society, it is important to throw light on at least two different aspects of working life:

a.   What occupations do people have?
b.   Where are places of work located?

By closely following the development of an agrarian parish during the transformation of Sweden from an agrarian to an industrial society, this particular part of the project will also help us to understand the present situation.

2. The Basis for Physical Planning

The landscape of today can be understood only if we utilize a long-term time perspective and a well-defined concept of the spatial structure of society and the forces causing its development. The landscape of tomorrow is heavily restricted by that of today. The planning of the landscape ought to be based on a general picture of man and his environment and the Man-Landscape and Society Information System enables us to delimit different types of systems concerning working life, physical structure, organizational forms etc. These systems can be followed over a long period of time and *ought to be one of the main objects of study in the physical planning of the landscape.* The aim, then, is to show how such "systems" in an agrarian society originate, how they change and how they can be used in physical planning. Special attention will be paid to a discussion of terms, methods of collecting and using data and the delimitation of systems.

3. The Structure of Domains and the Cultural Landscape

One important, and little studied, aspect of the development of the cultural landscape is the structure of domains. The organizational form of an area not only influences the cultural landscape but also demographic development and, hence, living conditions as they are expressed in the form of ownership or the usage of arable land.

Within this framework, we intend to use the Man-Land information system in order to answer the following two questions:

a.   What is the significance of the structure of domains in relation to demographic development and living conditions?
b.   What is the effect of changes in the structure of domains upon the cultural landscape?

4. Living Conditions and the Development of the Landscape: some village examples from Locknevi

As has been stated above, much has been written on the subject of technical innovations and its relationship to population expansion. As our theoretical point of departure is the causes of population growth and its consequences, we shall present and analyse the histories of a series of Locknevi villages in order to answer the following questions:

a. Does population growth precede arable land expansion or *vice versa*?
b. Within which strata did the 18–19th century population growth take place; and do increases in different strata have different effects upon land-use?
c. Do different forms of land ownership lead to different population and land-use patterns?

5. Land Reforms as Societal Change Factors

Surprisingly little has been written on the subject of Swedish land reforms and their effects upon society. Most investigations have been conducted on the regional level, and have mainly concerned the spread of the reforms and, more superficially, their implementation on the village level. Thorough village descriptions are few and far between, although Sigurd Erixon's "Kila – an Ostrogothian forest village" is one frequently-mentioned example. The effects of the land reforms on the local level (especially of the 'laga skifte' and 'enskifte', the more radical reforms) are not yet depicted anywhere.

Historical geographic studies of the late 18th and 19th centuries are few – despite the mass of high-quality data available. Studies of landscape development usually consider only the times up to the 'skifte' and take little or no account of one of the central aspects: the actors (people in large or small groupings) and their actions. One of the main reasons for neglecting this period – most important for understanding Swedish society of today – may be that the enormous amount of data available requires computer processing for the proper analysis and evaluation of the development process. another reason may be that a methodological shift has since occurred; from superficial, cross-sectional analysis to process analysis on an individual level.

The main aim of this project is to fill in some of the gaps in our knowledge concerning 18th and 19th century development in relation to the agrarian land reforms. By studying some spatial domains and their inhabitants in detail over a period of 50 years or more with the accent on the decade of the 'laga skifte', and by considering ownership patterns, population patterns, demographic development, social development and resource transfer from one generation to another, we hope to provide satisfying answers to certain questions. The main research questions will be: What were the consequences of the total transfer of common land to the different free-holders? Did all social groups remain intact or were the crofters and cottagers, whose positions were clearly threatened, expelled from their local systems and replaced by the free-holders' children? Can the 'skifte' reform be seen as a major 'push' factor behind the rural-urban population flow of the 19th century, which was obviously dominated by the landless? What effects did it have upon the enclosed domain and its social and spatial structure?

V. EDUCATIONAL DEVELOPMENT IN SWEDEN – AN OVERVIEW

A. Compulsory education in Sweden

Compulsory education in Sweden has quite a long history. The teaching of reading on a large scale had already begun by the 1650's and tests of reading knowledge were regularly administered by the Church in many parishes ("husförhör" = Church examination). This reading education was made compulsory for the entire population by the Church Law of 1686.

The aim of compulsory reading education, and especially the 1686 Church Law, was to extend the influence of the "hustavla" among the peasantry. As Johansson (1977) points out, "the Church Law contained rulings about general literacy. It said, for example, that children, farm-hands and maid-servants should learn to read and see with their own eyes what God bids and commands in His Holy World. This expression is typical of the Reformation: every individual was to see 'with his own eyes' and thus learn the meaning of the Bible". What the landless were supposed to understand was obviously the strict *social* order of the "hustavla" (see Diagram 9), which can be said to have been a means for *social* and *spatial* control of the people by the Church and the Sovereign (see Pleijel 1970).

After the Church Law of 1686 and the Conventicle Edict of 1726, which consisted of complementary principles and orders, the *reading* ability of the Swedish population increased steadily. By 1800, around 90 per cent of the adult population was literate (see Johansson 1977). Teaching took place in the home and was the responsibility of the head of the family. Reading ability was also tested annually in the home by the parish rector.

A by-product of these home-examinations were the Church examination registers, the foundation of the famous Swedish system of population registration. In the 17th century, the main objective of the registers was to record the reading and memorizing ability of the peasantry but *not* usually demographic changes between the yearly examinations such as migration, births, deaths, marriages and so on. Thus, the registers were generally made up for each examination in the form of a Catechism protocol, and are of limited value in population research. Beginning in the mid 18th century, however, demographic details were included, giving the registers a twofold function. From this time, then, the registers represent a continuous record of all demographic events – in some places this type of registration began even earlier, for example in the diocese of Västerås (see Diagram 10 and Åkerman 1978). Each volume was used for two to fifteen years, and comprised the population register of one parish. Newcomers and emigrants were recorded as well as the births, marriages, communions, deaths and migration inside the parish. For each house examination (generally one in each hamlet per annum), the reading and memorizing marks as well as the rector's intelligence ratings of his parishioners were noted for everyone present. Those not present were also recorded, along with presence at Holy Communion in Church (see Diagram 11–13). With complementary birth, death, marriage, communion and migration registers, the population book-keeping of the Swedish Church provides a marvellous opportunity for population research.

The "hustavla", a religious plague which was hung on the wall, was a supplement to Martin Luther's Little Catechism. It consisted of specific Bible verses arranged according to the traditional Lutheran doctrine of a three-stage social hierarchy - - - ecclesia (the Church), politia (the State) and oeconomia (the home or household). These selections of Scripture outlined the Christian duties and obligations which each stage in the hierarchy owed to the other two - - - i.e. priests / parishioners, teachers / pupils, rulers / subjects, heads of families / children and household servants.

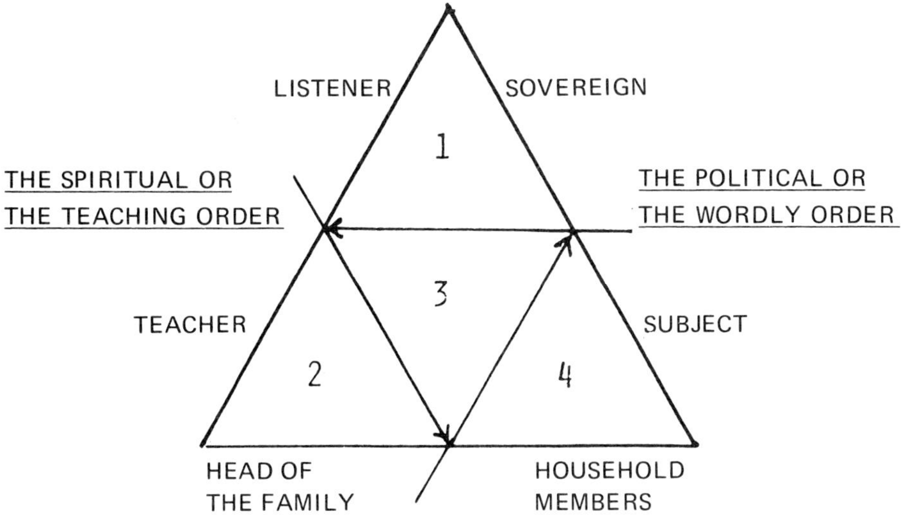

According to the code of the "Hustavla", everybody lived in a three-dimensional system of social relations. The diagram can be made more concrete by means of the following examples:

1. The king was sovereign in the political, listener in the spiritual and head of the family in the economic order.

2. The clergyman was correspondingly subject, teacher and head of the family.

3. The master was a subject in the country, listener in the congregation and head of the family in this house.

4. The rest were, generally speaking, subjects, listeners and household members.

Diagram 9. The social order of the "HUSTAVLA". Source: Johansson (1977) pp. 12–13.

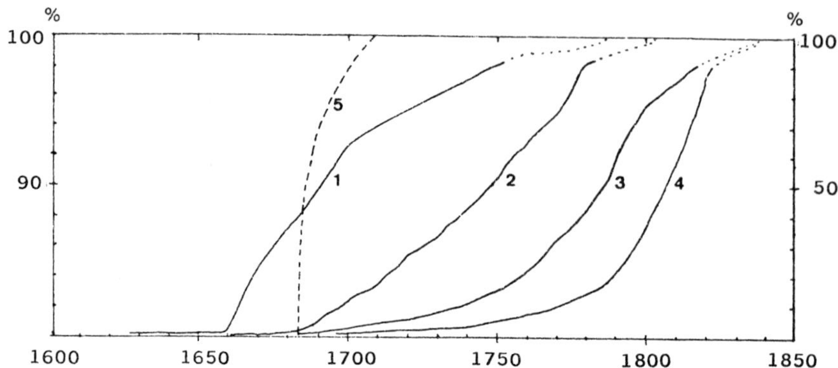

Diagram 10. The oldest preserved Church examination registers for every countryside parish in Sweden (N = 2373). The figure also includes Catechism registers for the diocese of Lund (N=424). Percentage figures for dioceses.

1 = the diocese of Västerås
2 = the dioceses of Härnösand, Uppsala, Strängnäs, Karlstad, Växjö and Visby
3 = the dioceses of Linköping, Kalmar, Skara and Gothenburg

4 = the diocese of Lund
5 = the diocese of Lund, Catechism registers.

(Source: Johansson (1977) p. 23).

The second main period of educational expansion (see Paulston 1976), occurred during the first half of the 19th century. Voluntary elementary schools were already in operation by 1800, but it was not until after the Elementary School Act was passed in 1842 that every parish was obliged to arrange elementary education, at the very latest by 1847. All children did not have to attend school regularly however, and those who were poor could obtain an almost complete dispensation. This was also the case if the tuition provided in the home was considered adequate by the vicar or by the schoolmaster. Church representatives generally played a major part in the local school boards until the early 20th century.

School attendance was at first very low, especially among children living far from school or belonging to the landless and poor, but the situation gradually improved as a result of a series of complementary reforms passed during the second half of the 19th century. By 1910, school participation had reached a level regarded as acceptable by the national school authorities. In later sections, we shall examine both the pattern of school establishment and the pattern of recruitment to elementary education in more detail (see Sections V:C and D and Chapters VI and VII).

Initially, the content of elementary schooling was dominated by religious instruction and the teaching of basic skills — writing and mathematics — although girls could be exempted from mathematics. Children were expected to be able to read before starting elementary school at 6 to 8 years of age, as a result of previous home education. Not until the establishment of preparatory schooling between 1860 and 1880 was reading supposed to be learnt at school. It is obvious, though, that the pupils' reading ability upon beginning school was usually very poor. Different political groupings in society ascribed different aims to the elementary school reform. Liberals such as Torsten Rudenschöld (see Rudenschöld 1845 and 1846) saw elementary education as an equalizer between social strata and as a means for social circulation. Conservatives such as the representatives of the Church saw elementary schooling as a means of regaining control over the

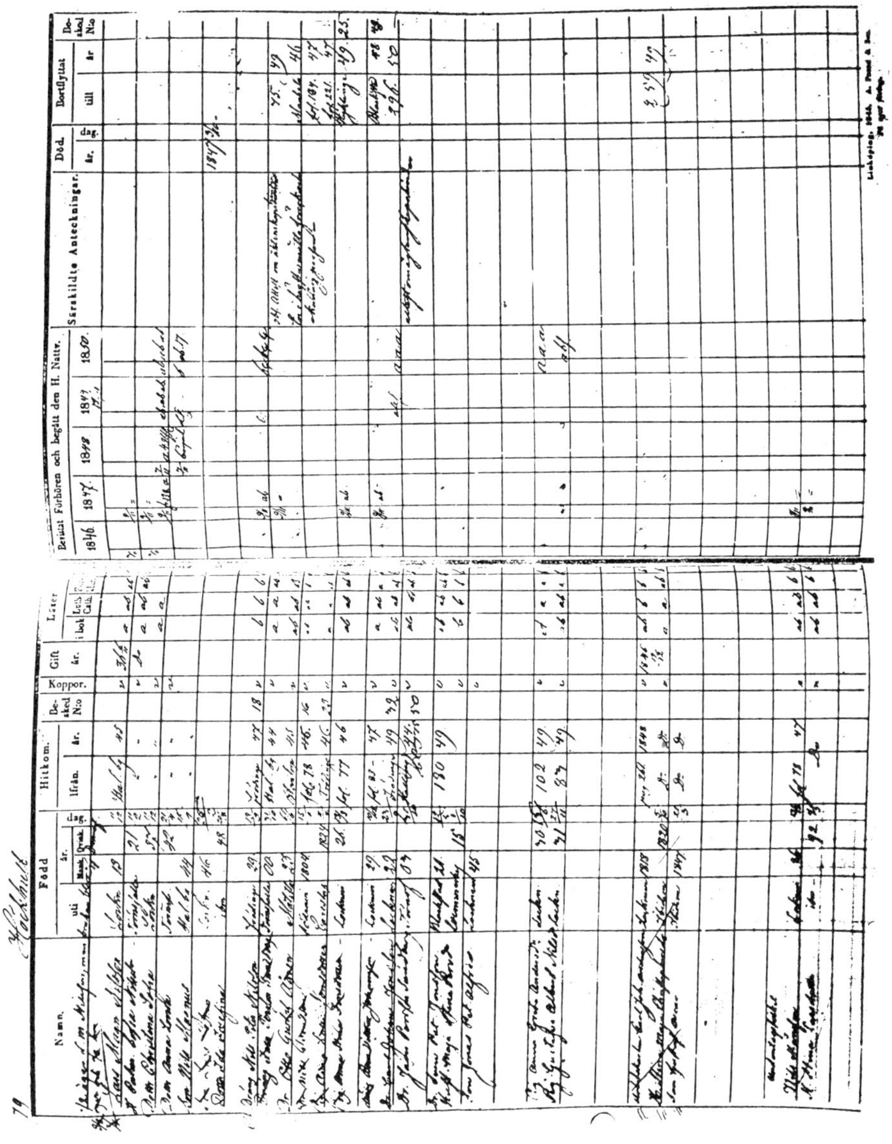

Diagram 11. A Church examination register for the Hamlet of Höckhult, Locknevi parish, 1846–1850.

92 (PAGE) LÖNNEBERGA PARISH   DIOCESE OF LINKÖPING

ÅKARP (NAME OF HAMLET)

SNARBRÄTEN (NAME OF DWELLING) NAMES	BORN YEAR	BORN DAY	PARISH OF BIRTH	ARRIVED YEAR	ARRIVED FROM	MARRIED YEAR	MARRIED DAY	SMALLPOX VACC.	READS THE BIBLE	READS LUTHER'S CATECHISM	READS EXPLANATIONS	UNDERSTANDS	1846 DAY	1846	1847 DAY	1847	1848 DAY	1848	1849 DAY	1849	1850 DAY	1850	NOTES	DEAD YEAR	DEAD DAY	MIGRATED YEAR	MIGRATED TO	CERTIFICATE NR
~~CROFTER OLOF OLOFSSON~~	1815	12/7	FRÖDINGE	1840	PAGE 22	1840	3/7	v.	a	a	a	ab	4/12	ab			5/12	ab			24/11	ab				1850	VIMMERBY	32
WIFE KARIN JOHANSDOTTER	1812	1/10	LÖNNEBERGA	1840	PAGE 41	"	"	v.	ab	+	+	+	4/12	+			5/12	+			24/11	+						
SON JOHAN	1841	3/12	"					v.	ab	ab	ab	+									24/11	ab						
DAUGHTER MARIA	1843	26/2	"					v.																				
DAUGHTER ANNA	1845	10/9	"					v.																1849	1/10			
DAUGHTER KARIN	1847	17/5	"					v.																				
CROFTER LARS JANSSON	1821	25/5	PELARNE	1850	PAGE 155			v.																				
~~MAID SARA SVENSDOTTER~~	1830	16/7	LÖNNEBERGA	1846	PAGE 43			v.	a	a	a	a	4/12	a												1847	FRÖDINGE	10
~~MAID NINA ANDERSDOTTER~~	1834	18/2	HÄSSLEBY	1847	HÄSSLEBY			v.	+	+	+	c					5/12	+								1849	VIMMERBY	23
MAID GRETA PETERSDOTTER	1836	9/11	RUMSKULLA	1849	PAGE 110			v.	+	+	+	+									24/11	+						

Diagram 12. Schematic outline of a page in a Church examination register.

1858.   Utflyttade

Dat.	N:o	Namn	Från	Till	Man kön	Qvin kön
				Transp.	25	19
14/5	16.	Gossen Carl Bernhard (alföljd N: 15.)	Toperum	Gottheborg	1	—
17/6	17	Hustr. Carolina Sof. Andersdtr	Mantobe	Hjorthed	—	1.
17/6	18	Hustrun Christina Maria Olofsdtr	Sjöstugan	Frödinge	—	1.
1/9	19.	Pig. Christina Sofia Westergren	Hund	Eksiö Landsförs.	—	1.
22/9	20	Hustrun Clara Wilhelmina Svensdtr	Stenbäcken	Westervik	—	1.
26/9	21.	Dr. Sven Pet. Elg	Emtebo	Odensvi	1	—
27/10	22	Dr. Anders J. Niklasson	Emmedal	D:o	1	—
	23	Kusken Lind med hushåll	Lidhem	Torgatorp	1	2
	24	Pig. Sofia Ljung	d:o	Pelarna	—	1
	25	d:o Lovisa Ullman	d:o	Eksiö	—	1
	26	Johanna Lundgren	d:o	Kimmorrby	—	1.
	27	Christina Svensdotter	d:o	d:o	—	1
	28	Dr. Johan Aug. Svensson	Sporrbacka	Frödinge	1.	—
	29	Dr. Anders Pet. Andersson	Sandviken	Blackstad	1	—
	30	Pig. Anna Maria Johansdtr	Gjersfall	Frödinge	—	1
	31	Dr. Anders M. Nilsson	Kulhult	Hjorthed	1	—
	32	d:o And. Joh. Svensson	Aninge	Horn	1.	—
	33	Pig. Anna Lovisa Persdtr	Sågarestugan	Odensvi	—	1.
	34	d:o Albert Charl. Nyström	Herrefallan	d:o	—	1
	35	d:o Maja Lisa Månsdotter	Snarö	Hallingeberg	—	1
	36	Trädgårdsmäst. Barklund	Hvanstad	d:o	1	—
	37	Pig. Charlotta Svensdtr	Kråkenäset	Hycklinge	—	1.
	38	d:o Christ. Wilh. Andersdtr	Gunnersbo	Hjorthed	—	1
	39	d:o Maja Lena Andersdotter	Björkhult	Kråkshult	—	1
	40	d:o Maria Lov. Ljungström	Måleund	Ed.	—	1
	41	d:o Christ. Charl. Jonsdtr	Orrhult	Blackstad	—	1
	42	d:o Christina Sof. Nilsdotter	Gärdsränga	Odensvi	—	1.
	43	Ynglingen Otto Horsvall	Råhult	d:o	1	—
	44	Pig. Carolina Andersdotter	d:o	Ed	—	1
	45	d:o Carolina Nilsdotter	d:o	Loftahammar	—	1
	46	Spikhsmed Anders Grönberg	Toperum	Wimmerby	1	3.
	47	Dr. Joh. Fr. Lundstedt	d:o	d:o	1	—
	48	d:o Gustaf Ad. Tyr	d:o	Lofta	1	—
	49	Pig. Anna Sof. Månsdtr	d:o	Blackstad	—	1
	50	Dr. Adch. Lanström med hustr.	Malen	d:o	1	2
	51	Dr. Carl Aug. Ericsson	Orrhult	Ukna	1	—
	52	Pig. Lena Jaensdtr	Kjerka	Hallingeberg	—	1
	53	Smeden Carl G. Bengström	Toperum	Torgatorp	3.	2
	54	Hammarsmeden Syl. med hushåll	d:o	Alfvested	1	2
	56	Smeddräng Fredrich Solberg	d:o	Stenbäcken	1.	—
	55	d:o Per G. Hasberg	d:o	d:o	1	—
		99			45	52

Diagram 13. An emigration register for Locknevi parish, 1858.

42

people – the social order of the "hustavla" has become somewhat absolete in the stress-ful situation resulting from the rapid population growth and proletarianization of the early 19th century.

The most recent major reform in the field of compulsory education has been the establishment of the 9-year elementary school ("grundskola") in the 1950's and 1960's. The aim of this reform was the achievement of educational uniformity – different types of parallel schools were amalgamated into one so that everyone should have the same basic education. This reform also had a *social* aim – the school was to be used as an instrument for the achievement of greater social equality and social justice in society as a whole (see Dahllöf 1971 and Richardson 1977). The educational planners apparently still saw education as a "Great Equalizer" and not as a conservative force (see Anderson 1962).

A change in official attitudes is evident from the time of the Church Law of 1686 through the elementary school reform of 1842 until the "grundskola" reform of 1957. The aim of the Church Law was social control of the people by the Church and the Sovereign; the aim of the 1842 reform represented a compromise between the conservative "social controllers" (Church and Nobility) and the liberal (or humanistic) "social circulators"; while the aim of 1957 was expressed as equality and social justice.

B. The development of voluntary education

Higher education has also undergone a series of reforms, generally organizational in nature, since 1945. Upper secondary ("gymnasium") education had begun by 1623, but until the beginning of the 20th century, only 2 to 4 per cent of most age-cohorts went on to higher education.

The development of gymnasia in Sweden between 1850 and 1970 is illustrated in Maps 12–14. As *recruitment* to higher education is the main factor considered here, we shall not describe the reforms in detail. However, it is important to examine the *dispersion* of educational units during this time so that we can relate individual recruitment to different levels and types of education with the spatial and hierarchical structure of the educational system.

Of special interest in the present context is the increased enrolment in gymnasia, vocational schools, colleges and universities. Between 1900 and 1965 (when the new comprehensive gymnasium was introduced) enrolment increased from about 5 per cent to 25 per cent of an age-cohort (Gesser 1971) without any more radical reform on the national level. The greatest change in the pattern of recruitment came in the 1940's, when recruitment began to increase at around 8 per cent per annum. Such growth was possible because of the greatly increased capacity of higher education, measured both in terms of the number of units and the capacity of the individual unit (see Ekstedt 1976; Hoppe 1974; Pålsson 1958).

Expansion on the university level occurred at a later point in time, largely because the minimum entrance requirement has generally been completion of gymnasium education. The number of universities as well as their size and capacity has also increased, mainly since 1965.

Running parallel to this more "academic" type of education is a professional training system which is becoming more and more formalized. Since 1971, the main components of this training have been included in the gymnasium as separate programs. More than 80 per cent of an age-cohort now passes on to some kind of voluntary higher education

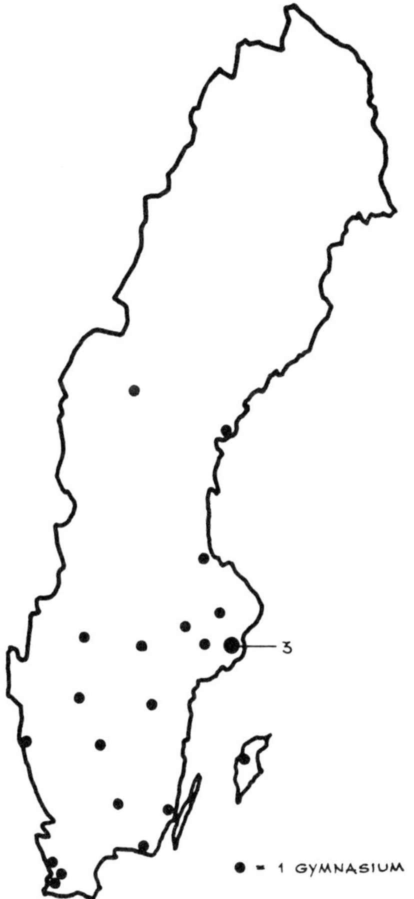

Map 12. Gymnasia in 1850.

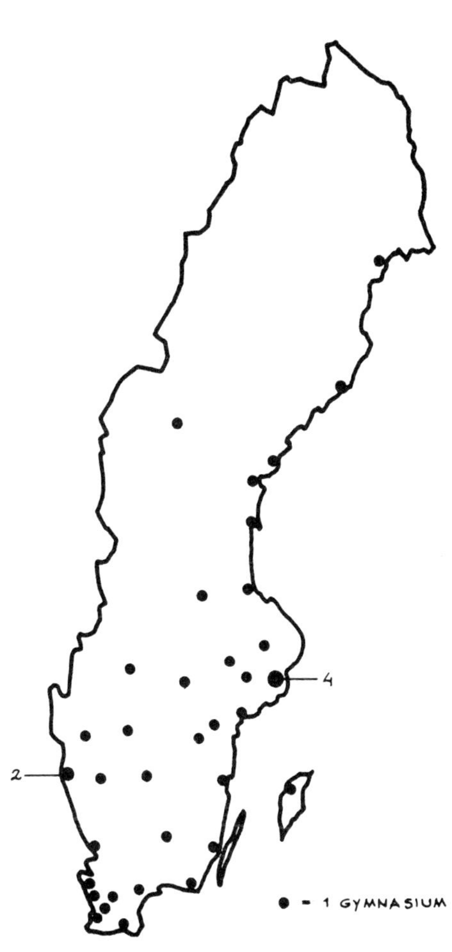

Map 13. Gymnasia in 1910.

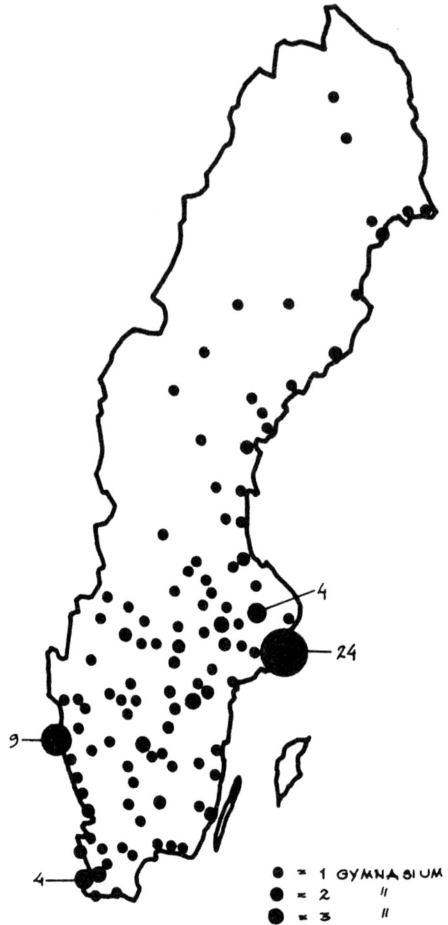

Map 14. Gymnasia in 1972.

mentioned, many other types of education (some partly parallel) are also available. Examples of a more non-vocational nature are the "folkhögskola" (Peoples' high schools); examples of professional (and paid) training are police and military (officers) training or nursing courses. The number of students participating in "folkhögskola" and this type of professional education has also been rising in recent years.

Map 15 illustrates the pattern of gymnasium establishment in the region surrounding Locknevi. As can be seen, the establishment of gymnasia intensified here during the 20th century, especially after 1940. If we want to use individual and longitudinal data on life-paths which include at least part of the active life outside education, changes in the educational system which have taken place in the last 10 years cannot be included in the analysis. This is because the life-paths for individuals born after 1950 would not be long enough. All gymnasia shown on Map 15 have potentially been open to the population studied although, in reality, most people attended the Västervik or Hultsfred gymnasia because of their proximity. Other types of education on the intermediary level, professional schooling, people's high schools etc. were also available fairly close to Locknevi, e.g. in Vimmerby and Gamleby.

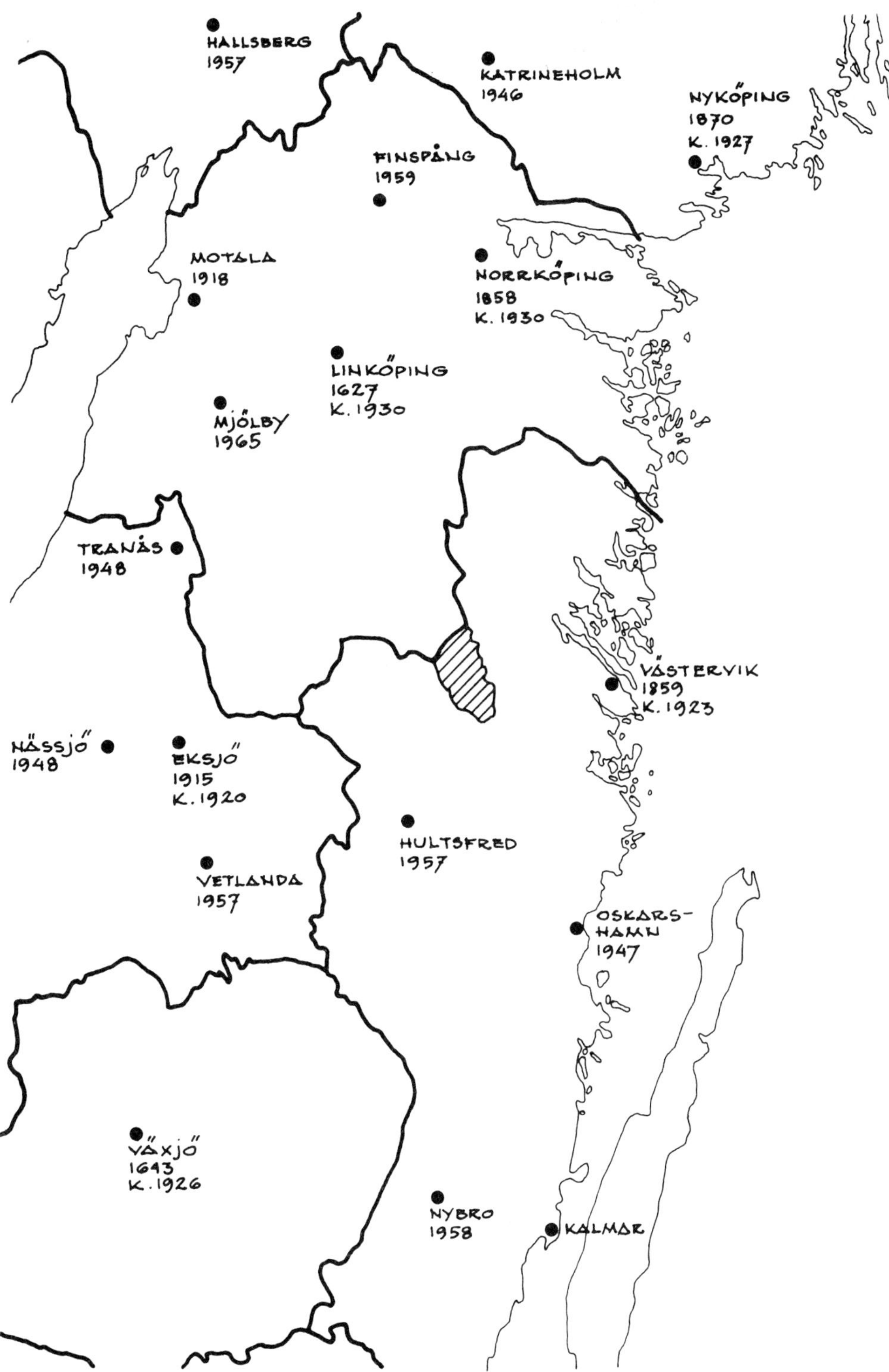

Map 15. The pattern of gymnasia establishment in the region surrounding Locknevi.

C. Elementary school establishment on a local level —
   The case of Locknevi parish

In this section, we shall describe the development of school units using as an example a local parish — Locknevi. The description will largely follow the minutes of the school board and parish meetings of Locknevi and will be accompanied by maps and other illustrations.

1. The initial stage

After the passing of the Elementary School Act in 1842, the curate-in-charge called a parish meeting in November to inform the parishioners of the Act and to decide on further local school policy. From the minutes, we can follow the proceedings:

> " § 8   In order to follow His Royal Majesty's gracious statute of the 18th of June on popular education in the Kingdom, as well as the Reverend Cathedral Chapter's letter to the parish were given notice of the necessity of deciding on the foundation of an Elementary School inside Locknevi and on this urgent matter decided:
>
> 1. That a so-called Permanent School shall be organized inside the Parish. The most suitable location for the same was considered to be in the vicinity of the Church, or on the premises of the Vicar's Residence, if possible.
>
> 2. That the School Board, besides the Vicar or the curate-in-charge, shall consist of six members of the parish elected as follows: Chamber Chancellor The Right Honourable Eggert Elers, the Ironworks Proprietor The Honourable Baltzar De Maré, Lieutenant The Honourable Gustaf Edgard von Breitholtz of the Hvanstad Estate, Freeholder Jonas Jönsson in Östankärr, Freeholder Carl Magnus Jonsson in Wrångfall and Freeholder Carl Magnus Jonsson in Gård-spånga. This School Board shall immediately go into operation with the making of proposals for the building of the school-house and the preparation of the expedient organization of the School and will this School Board, without any change of its members, continue in action until at least one year after the school has been legally established.
>
> 3. That the future school-master's pay will be paid in the way that the Royal Act § 4 Moment 4 recommends, with a fee from every registered parishioner and also with a fee from the wealthier children that use the school."

(From the minutes of the parish meeting of November 2, 1842.)

We can see that the landed strata dominated the school board completely. Not one single cottar or crofter was elected to the Board although their number at the time was large, at least 50 per cent of the parishioners. The Nobility (including the parish rector) was in the majority. It is quite interesting to notice that the iron-works proprietor of Toverum, who lived in Ankarsrum, ten miles from Locknevi, suddenly became a parishioner. After this meeting and school board election, an entire year passed without any educational activities at all. There was probably no hurry, as each parish had five years from 1842 in which to build a school and begin tuition. In November 1843, the parishioners gathered in order to decide on a location for the school. In fact, no location was selected and instead the entire proceedings were postponed with the following statement:

" § 9   A written statement was delivered with the following text: 'After what was decided earlier on the matter of a School building in Locknevi, we, the undersigned (17 persons) want to make known the following: Firstly that we do not see any reason for taking such extreme measures with buildings and other coming actions, as we already have a school-master in the parish who circulates for one month in each hamlet and then instructs the children in religious matters, and to engage more than one school-master in such a small parish, with so many poor inhabitants, would be the way to certain ruin. And if a postponement can be obtained until the next Parliamentary session, we are almost certain that the School Act will come to nothing, as there are already many parishes which do not concern themselves with any building for this purpose but rely themselves on the fact that this project will not be permanent. It can certainly put Locknevi into more troublesome circumstances than other neighbouring parishes, as we have a school-master with whom we are satisfied. If this is not approved of, we think that the parish cottage could be used for education during weekdays and, for the school-master's dwelling, there are rooms in the poor-house. Secondly, if all children in the parish between 8 and 15 years of age shall study, who is then to do the work? Those years are quite the best working years, to train the working people. If those years are gone, the love of work is gone too. What will be then? A great misery for the future!' "

(From the minutes of the parish meeting of November 13, 1843.)

Apparently, the aforementioned conservative powers of society did not see the school only as a means of control, at least not on this local level. The statement cited above was supported by many of those present at the meeting and the building of a school was postponed for two years. In 1845, though, a building committee was appointed and it was decided that the poor-house by the parish Church should be enlarged, and that the second floor should be used as a school and schoolmaster's dwelling. In January 1946, however, this decision was over-roled and the school board now decided upon a new building. The progression of the building is described as follows:

" § 7   The parish was presented with projects and designs for a School House building, either an enlargement of the poor-house or a new building. The parish left the earlier decision on an enlargement of the poor-house and instead decided upon building a new School according to the design and the estimate now presented, which documents will now be kept in the Church for future access and guidance.

" § 8   According to the decision of the parish meeting of the 28th of July, now to be on offer were the following parts, all belonging to the completion of the new school-building:

Moment 1: The setting of the masonry. According to the contract that was read and intended for mutual guidance, the master bricklayer Johan Erik Stänholm of Österhult, Kulhult, undertook this task for a sum of 31 Riksdaler Banco.

Moment 2: The laying of the roof-boards as well as the working of the roof band. This work starts on Monday the 31st of this month and the Entrepreneur, for his daily assistance, will have 6 parish day-works. The boards on the

48

roof are properly edged and are lain double. The work was accepted by the Crofter Anders of Herrefälla, Björka for a sum of 20 shillings Riksgälds.

Moment 3: The Completion of the Windows and the Doors. The timber is chosen from that already delivered. The Windows will be three panes high and are to be deposited in their places with their wainscots and their mossings etc., as well as the Doors with their joints and mossings. The Doors are to be common panel doors. Of this work, the Doors and the Windows in the two rooms to the right on the ground floor are to be completed by the 15th October and installed. This work was accepted by the Crofter Anders of Herrefälla for a sum of 2.16 Riksdaler Banco for every Window and 4.24 Riksdaler Banco for every Door as the timber for the Doors is delivered by himself.

Moment 4: The woodwork and interior fittings. The work was accepted by the crofter Anders of Herrefälla for 38 Riksdaler Banco.

(From the minutes of the parish meeting of August 18th, 1846.)

By the summer of 1847, the Crofter Anders had completed his work and the school building was ready. Tuition could commence in the autumn semester of 1847. In the same year, the first regulations for the Locknevi schools were approved by the Cathedral Chapter of Linköping. Tuition was to take place every weekday except Saturdays from 8 a.m. to 6 p.m. Thus, compulsory elementary education in Locknevi was established.

The first school of Locknevi.

2. The growth stage

In order to build a reasonable spatial structure for the local educational system, the school board was permitted to divide the parish into appropriate squads or "stations". In Locknevi, four school districts were constructed — the Church station, the Wrångfall station, the Toverum station and the Ytterbo station (see Map 16) — and these districts remained intact until the schools were forced to close down. Part of the aim of this sub-division was, of course, to minimize the daily travelling of the children.

From the beginning the parish sexton also acted as a school-master, as there were not enough qualified teachers for every parish. He taught the children of the different school districts for a couple of months every year. In the district without a school building, tuition usually took place in the home of a freeholder. In the mid-1850's, two teachers — one qualified and one not — were engaged because the parish sexton no longer had time to do the job. One of the teachers was engaged for the Vrångfall and Toverum districts, the other one for Locknevi and Ytterbo. In 1864, elementary school inspectors were introduced and Locknevi's "entrepreneurial" educational development came under their direction. Table 1 summarizes the actions of the inspectors and the local school board for the 19th century; Diagram 14 depicts the number of school-masters engaged; while Map 17 shows the hamlets where teaching took place during the 19th century. As we can see, the school board often failed to respond to complaints made by the inspectors, for example those concerning the engagement of new teachers or the building of a school house. Only when the faults were easy (and inexpensive) to correct did the board respond.

In 1915, a second permanent school was opened in the Locknevi school district at Spillinge, while the permanent school of Vrångfall was finally built in 1926 after 75 years of education in a variety of temporary premises. With the building of these schools, the growth stage in Locknevi's educational development ended. At least one permanent school had been built in each district and preparatory classes were also in operation in every district.

Map 16. The school districts of Locknevi parish.

50

**Table 1. Locknevi School Board actions resulting from complaints
by the county elementary schools inspector**

Year	Type of complaint	Recommended action	School Board reaction
1864	*Buildings*	Repair the Church school at Locknevi.	Repairs to be done next summer.
1866	*Quality of tuition*	Non-literate children are not to be taught with the literates.	Literate children to be taught three days a week and non-literates the other two.
	School-attendance	The irregular schoolattendance must be improved.	One member of the School Board is to visit the schools once a week.
	Equipment	Proper reading books must be used instead of the Bible.	50 copies of Siljeström's reader to be bought.
1872	*Personnel*	Engage another qualified teacher.	Two teachers engaged 1875–80.
1873			Toverum's permanent school completed.
1875			Ytterbo permanent school completed.
1882	*Buildings*	Arrange for four permanent schools.	No action.
	Personnel	Engage another two qualified teachers.	No action.
	Buildings	Build four preparatory schools.	No action.
	Tuition	Increase teaching time.	No action.
1891	*Buildings*	Arrange for four permanent schools.	No action.
1892	*Personnel*	Engage more qualified teachers.	Another qualified teacher engaged in 1892.
	Tuition	Increase teaching time.	The number of annual school-days increased in all districts.
1894	*School-attendance*	The children of a certain family should attend schoool more frequently.	The school-master is to report to the School Board every two weeks on this matter.
1895	*School-attendance*	Increase school attendance during the potato harvest.	No action.
1896	*Tuition*	Arrange for female handiwork tuition.	No action.
	Tuition	Let the children of Vrångfall attend continuation courses at Locknevi.	No action.
1898	*Tuition*	Arrange for more continuation courses.	No action.
	Quality of tuition	Improve literacy in the first forms.	The children of the first forms may borrow the readers and read at home. School Board members are to visit the schools for control.
1899	*Tuition*	Arrange for continuation courses.	No action.

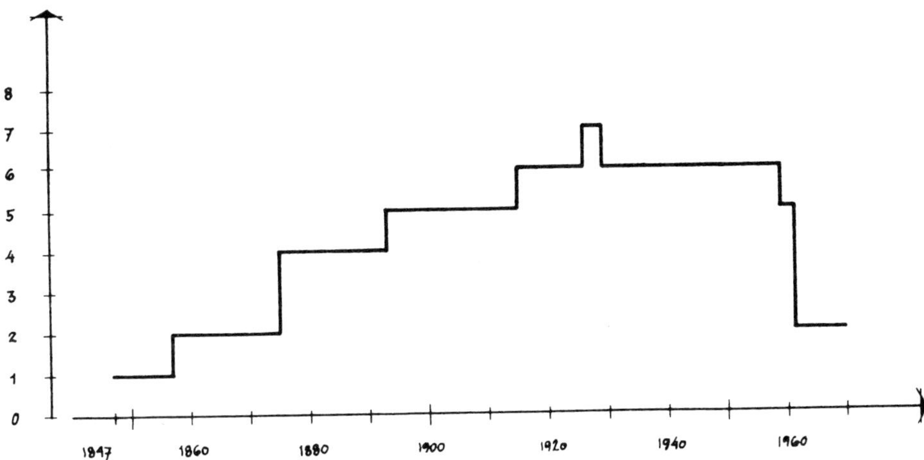

Diagram 14. The number of compulsory school teachers engaged in Locknevi parish, 1847–1980.

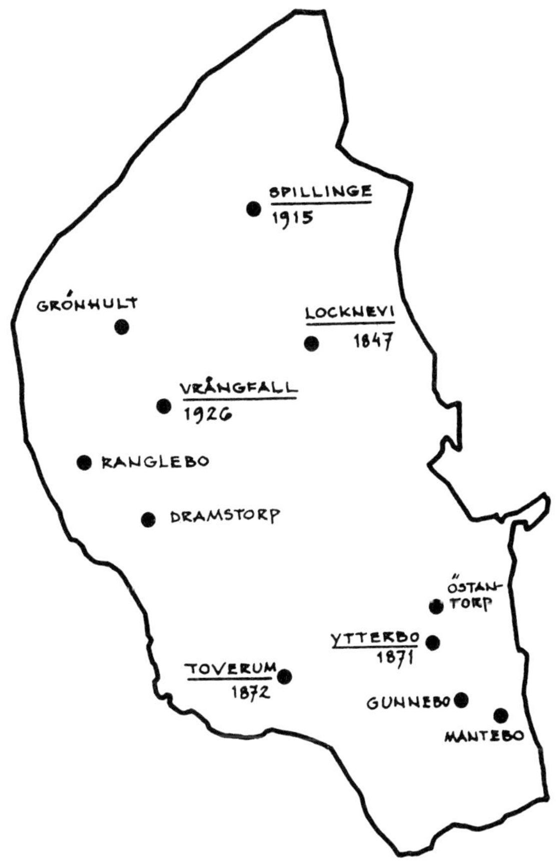

Map 17. Places where tuition took place in Locknevi. Underlined names indicate permanent schools and year of establishment.

Vrångfall's school built in 1926.

3. The regression stage

After 1930, the Spillinge school was closed down in response to the decreasing number of children in the district. This was the start of a "concentration" phase that still continues as the population of the parish decreases. Toverum's school was the next to go, in 1959, and in 1961 both the Vrångfall and Ytterbo schools were closed. The children had to go to the new "Central" school at Locknevi; a situation identical to that of 1847. Only two teachers were allowed to remain, all the others were dismissed. Today many of the children in Locknevi have to travel by bus to Frödinge or Vimmerby to attend school and, if the present trend continues, the school by the Church is also in severe danger of being closed, after 130 years of operation.

D. Elementary school establishment on the regional level
   — two examples

In order to cast further light upon compulsory school establishment, two studies on the regional level were also carried out (see Gerger 1974). The first was of the Mjölby-Boxholm area in central Östergötland and the second of the Southern Tjust area in the county of Kalmar, where Locknevi is situated (see Map 18). The purpose of these studies was to gain a more general knowledge of school location and establishment: was the pattern of school establishment and development found in Locknevi typical of the pattern for Sweden as a whole or were there differences between regions?

Map 18. The regions studied.

As a conceptual framework, we can use the general Hägerstrand model (Hägerstrand 1953 and 1967) of contagious innovation diffusion. This model consists of an initial phase, in which only a few people in a particular area accept an innovation; a growth stage in which less innovative neighbours begin to accept it more and more readily; a saturation stage where the innovation has been accepted by almost everybody and finally, a regression or concentration stage (see Nordström 1971; Gerger 1972) in which the use of the innovation begins to decrease. The introduction of schooling cannot be said to have been a true household innovation as defined in the Hägerstrand model but rather an entrepreneurial one (see Pedersen 1970 and 1971). For it was not until after the parish authorities had been forced to accept the School Act and the obligation to build schools that children could actually be sent to school (the household innovation).

We can also divide innovations into two types in terms of their character. On the one hand, we have innovations which are accepted quite voluntarily on both the entrepreneurial and household levels such as automobiles (see Hägerstrand 1953) or television (see Törnqvist 1967) and so on. On the other hand, we have innovations that are to some extent controlled or made compulsory by authorities on one particular level (national, regional or local). Examples of this kind of innovation are population registration or, as in our case, compulsory schooling.

The diffusion pattern of a controlled innovation will differ from that of a completely voluntary one both spatially and temporally. The compulsory School Act prescribed that every parish should build a school and introduce tuition by the year 1847, as was done in Locknevi parish. For the Mjölby-Boxholm region (see Map 19) the location pattern for 1847 can best be described as 'dispersed' as 20 of the 24 parishes in the area had one permanent school by this year. In 1848, another two parishes completed their first schools while the remaining two parishes, Malexander and Blåvik, opened their first schools in 1864 and 1896 respectively. It is significant that these last two parishes were also the most peripherally located.

Map 19. Schools in Mjölby-Boxholm area 1847/48.

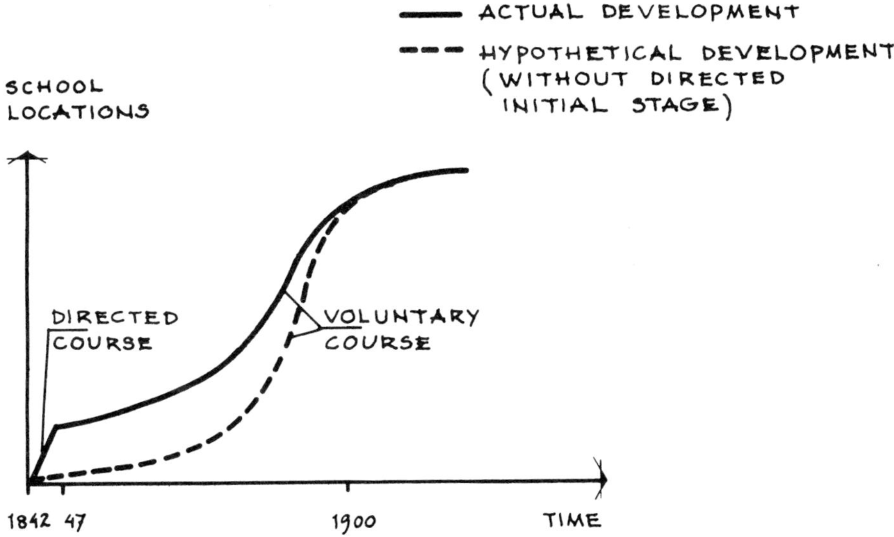

Diagram 15. Quantitative school development in an hypothetic area.

Hence, in spite of the School Act, the first acceptance stage was a prolonged one, not of the "ideal" type for a controlled innovation of an entrepreneurial type (see Diagram 15), but rather an intermediary between that and the completely voluntary type. The initial school establishment phase was characterized by the central location of schools in the parishes, often by the Church as in Locknevi. That pattern thus seems to be a general one.

The number of permanent schools grew rapidly during the 1860's and the 1870's, and also during the 1890's. As we have seen in our *local* example, the actions of the county compulsory school inspectors played an important part in school establishment and there is no reason to believe that the process was any different on the regional level. School establishment reached a peak in the late 1920's, by which time there were 46 permanent schools in function in Mjölby-Boxholm. We can thus describe the 1920's as a saturation stage.

As the population of the region began to decrease, local authorities, with the permission of the county school board, began to close down schools so that a concentration of school units took place. Diagram 16 illustrates the actual *number* of schools in the Mjölby-Boxholm area while Diagram 17 shows the life-span of *individual* school units. It appears that the last schools to be established were also the first to be closed down. This was the case in Locknevi too — those schools which were located in central positions remained centrally located over time because the depopulation occurred mainly on the former periphery, and the peripheral schools were the first to be closed. Furthermore, the process of parish amalgamation which began in 1952 meant that it was no longer necessary for every parish to maintain its central school and parishes began sharing schools instead. Nevertheless, the pattern of schools which remained in 1972 was still very similar to the 1847 pattern — the last stage corresponds to the initial stage of the diffusion process.

Map 20. Schools in Mjölby-Boxholm area 1890/91.

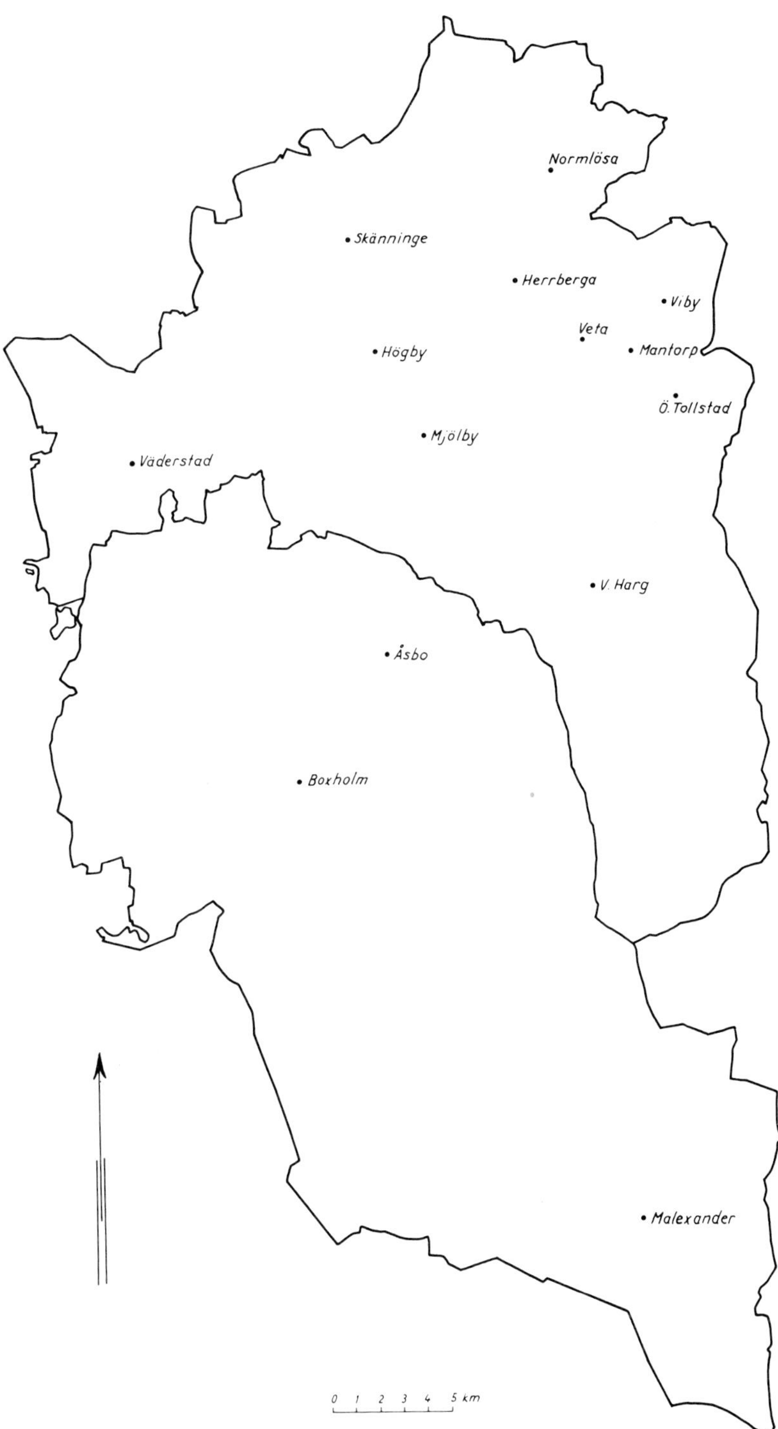

Map 21. Schools in Mjölby-Boxholm area 1971/72.

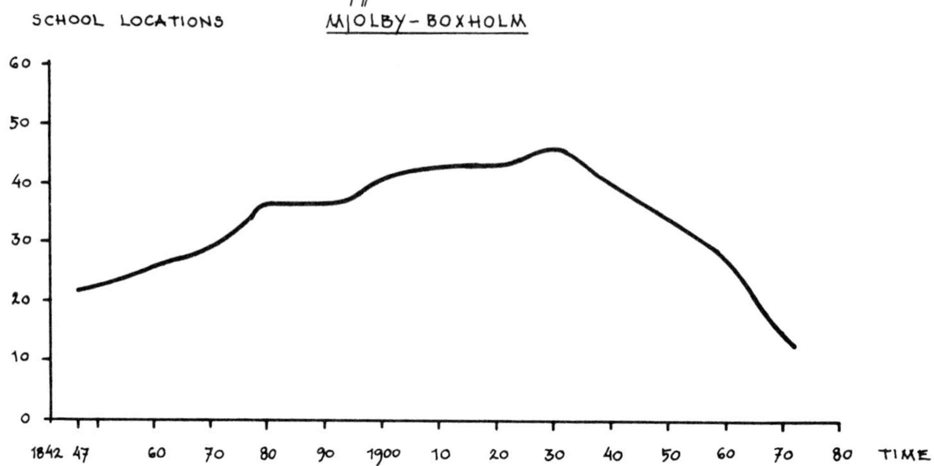

Diagram 16. Quantitative school development in the Mjölby-Boxholm area 1842–1970.

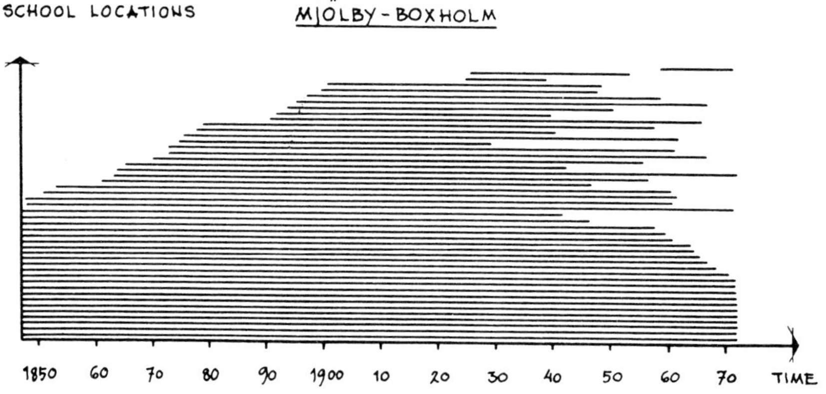

Diagram 17. Lifetime trajectories of the Mjölby-Boxholm area compulsory schools.

Our second study area — the Southern Tjust region — gave rise to a pattern rather similar to the one already described. The region consists of 11 parishes, all of which established their permanent school in 1847. Here the pattern differed somewhat in that the Tjust area is an ideal example of the initial stage of a completely controlled entrepreneurial innovation, as every parish fulfilled the conditions of the School Act. The growth stage was most intensive around 1880–90, somewhat *later* than in the Mjölby-Boxholm area. The maximum number of schools was reached around 1930 after which a rapid decline took place. The situation in the early 1970's was similar to that of the initial stage in 1847 — only a few relocations had taken place. The pattern of development is illustrated in Diagrams 18 and 19. The original units again survived the longest and are as centrally located today as they were in 1847.

The conclusions to be drawn from the regional studies in comparison with the local study are as follows:

1. The first school unit in each parish was centrally located. Thereafter, supplementary locations tended to be more and more peripheral in relation to the population distribution.

2. This gave rise to a general pattern where the pattern for the initial phase of the innovation was very similar to that of the concentration or regression phase, i.e. those units established in the periphery during the growth stage were also the first to disappear.

3. The slope of the diffusion curve in the acceptance and concentration phases differs from one region to another. Mjölby-Boxholm accepted schools more quickly, reached the maximum situation earlier and closed schools down more slowly than Southern Tjust. The differences in the concentration phase can be explained by the different patterns of population development in the two areas, but the different slopes of the curve in the acceptance phase require further explication.

One more reason for the high initial acceptance level (i.e. the large number of schools) in the area of Mjölby-Boxholm is that the parishes there were so small. Although Southern Tjust was no smaller in the total area, the number of parishes was not even half that of Mjölby-Boxholm. This meant that Mjölby-Boxholm already had quite an acceptable number of schools at the time when compulsory schooling was introduced. Hence a higher growth rate was needed in Southern Tjust, bearing in mind the fact that the population was no smaller than that in Mjölby-Boxholm. The reason for the small parishes in central Östergötland, as well as in all other "central" agrarian parts of Sweden was, of course, that these central areas were more densely populated (and taxated higher) when the parishes were originally laid out. The population of the central parishes in Sweden were thus probably similar to those of much larger parishes located in peripheral areas.

Map 22. Schools in Southern Tjust in 1847/48 (Gerger 1972).

Map 23. Schools in Southern Tjust in 1929/30 (Gerger 1972).

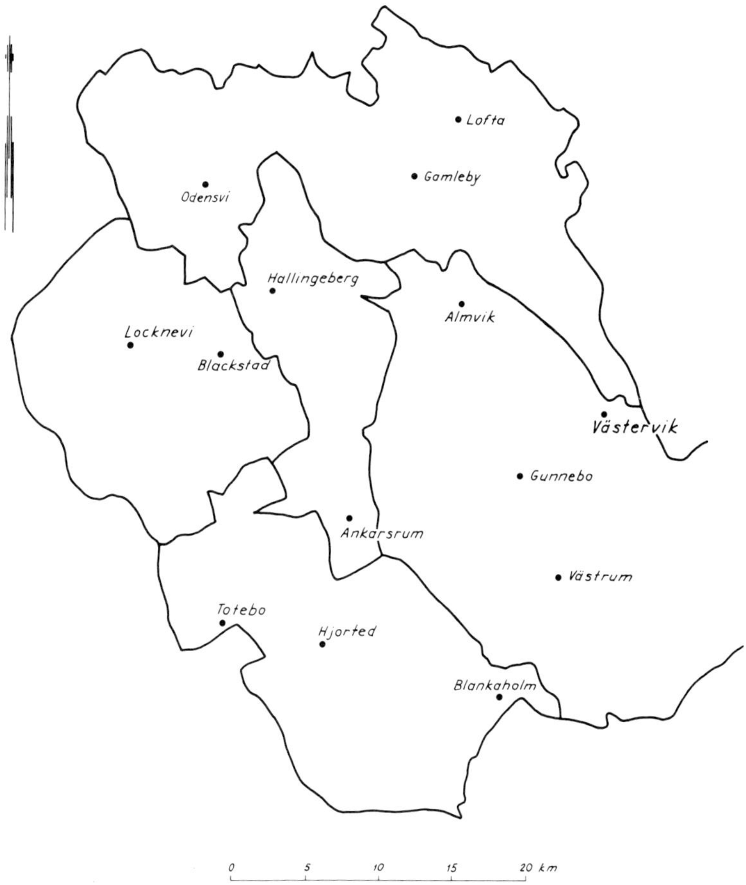

Map 24. Schools in Southern Tjust in 1972/73.

mnmnmnmnmnmnmnmnmnmnmnmnmnmnmnmnm

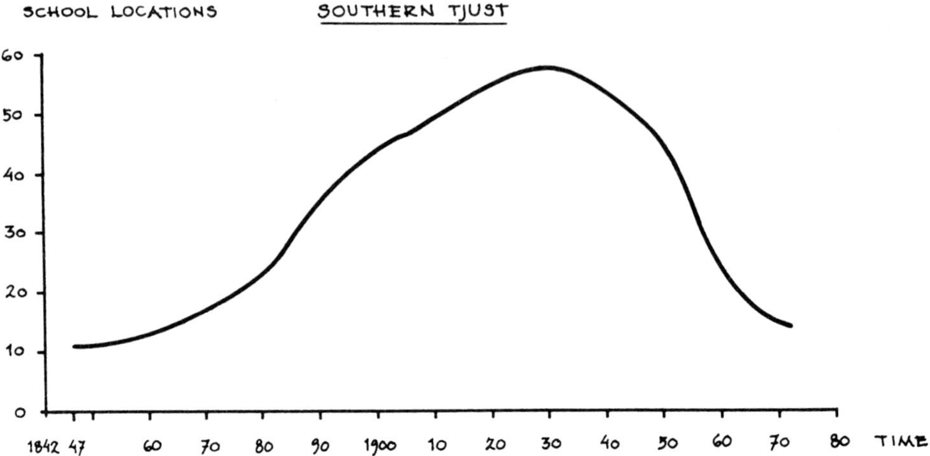

Diagram 18. Quantitative school development in the Southern Tjust area 1842–1970.

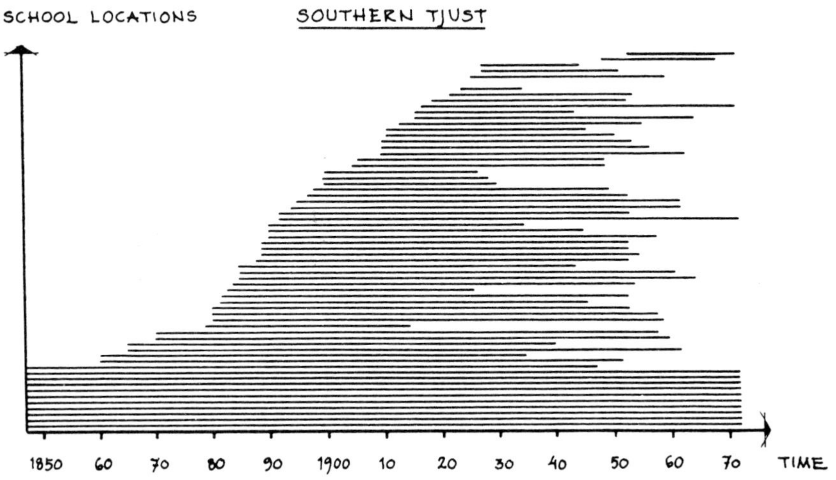

Diagram 19. Lifetime trajectories of the Southern Tjust area compulsory schools.

VI. RECRUITMENT TO EDUCATION: THE CASE OF LOCKNEVI 1847 TO 1965

This part of the book will have two main aims:

1. We want to *describe* recruitment to compulsory elementary education in the 19th century and to voluntary higher education in the 20th century.

2. We also want to *explain* the findings. The explanation will focus upon the differences in recruitment in terms of the background of the children.

We shall begin by presenting the results from the study of recruitment to elementary education and then pass on to recruitment of voluntary higher education.

The Theoretical Framework

First, however, it is necessary to develop a theoretical framework on the micro-level, involving factors derived from our knowledge of spatial diffusion processes. The acceptance of innovations is dependent upon two main groups of factors: the *information* we receive about the new cultural items and our *willingness* to accept them.

We maintain that the family decision to let children attend school is influenced by the factors illustrated in Diagram 20 in the following manner.

Factors	**Hypotheses**
Information	There is an indirect relationship between information received and school attendance. Thus, an increase in the positive information received from school authorities etc. tends to increase school attendance.
Economic resources	There is a direct relationship between economic resources and school attendance. Thus a high socio-economic status tends to increase school attendance.
Home environment	There is a direct relationship between home environment and school attendance. If the home environment is positive and supportive, then school attendance tends to increase.
The ability of the child	There is a direct relationship between the child's ability and school attendance. Thus high ability tends to increase school attendance or the converse.
Perceived benefits of education	There is a direct relationship between the perceived benefits of education and school attendance. If the benefits of education are perceived to be high, then school attendance tends to increase.
Physical environment	There is a direct relationship between position in the physical environment and school attendance. Thus a short distance between home and school tends to increase school attendance.

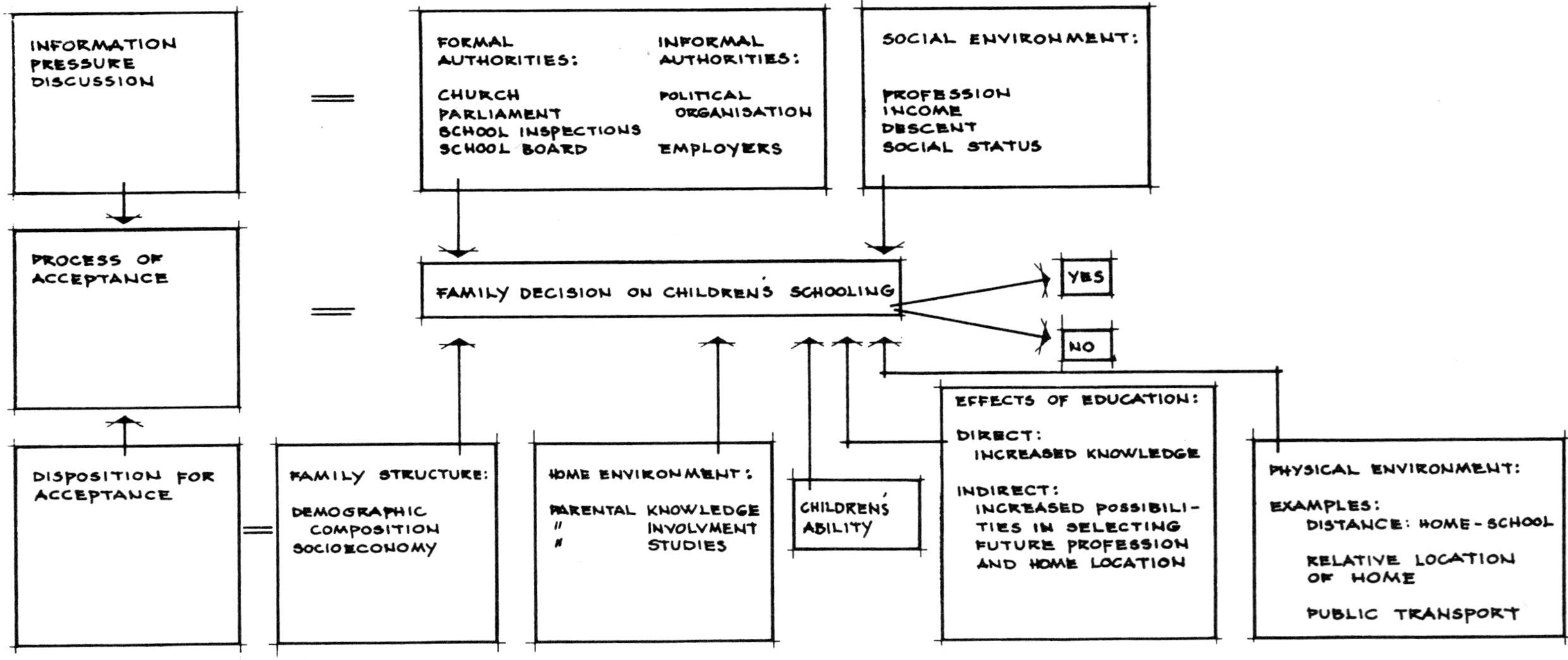

Diagram 20. Schematic outline of the schooling acceptance process.

School children from Vrångfall in the 1910s.

Pupils in Vrångfall Compulsory School around 1940.

Recruitment to Compulsory Elementary Education 1847—1900

The Sources

For our study we needed two kinds of information: a documentation of the population in the investigation area and a detailed documentation of school activities dating from the introduction of elementary education in Locknevi in 1847. To obtain the first we consulted the church registers which enabled us to trace all the people living in Locknevi parish, to "build" families, to classify them in terms of occupational status, to map where they lived and so on. These registers were described in Chapter V.

In the church archives of Locknevi, extraordinarily well-documented school registers were found which enabled us to follow day-by-day education in the parish, to see how many days the schools were open, to check which children went to school, what marks they received and so forth. Diagram 21 gives an overview of the sources used. We should also point out that throughout the years we have found these sources to be highly dependable.

The Study of School Attendance

The first step was to *describe* school attendance, and this was done according to the following five stages:

Which children should be investigated?	To which school district did they belong?	When were they supposed to go to school?	How many school days were offered per annum?	For how many days did children actually attend school?

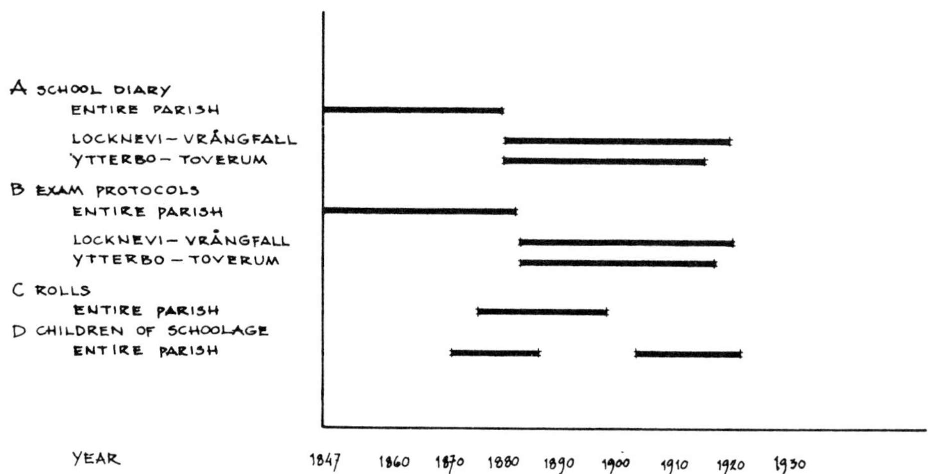

Diagram 21.

Table 2. Frequency distribution of age-cohorts.

Year of birth	Number of children in each cohort		Number of children in each cohort
1830	45	1844	46
1831	43	1845	41
1832	57	1846	66
1833	50	1847	47
1834	55	1848	69
1835	62	1849	63
1836	53	1850	52
1837	71	1851	46
1838	43	1852	60
1839	52	1853	55
1840	55	1854	77
1841	55	1870	67
1842	43	1880	40
1843	58	**Total population**	**1471**

1. The children investigated

From the Church registers we selected those children who lived in Locknevi while they were of school age and who were born i) between 1830 and 1854, ii) in 1870 and iii) in 1880. This demarcation allowed us to follow the development of elementary education in Locknevi during the first twenty years, as the children born in 1854 did not leave school until the end of the 1860's. It also allowed us to throw light upon the continued expansion of education which took place at the end of the century by following those born in 1870 and 1880. As Table 2 shows, the study was based on a population of nearly 1500 children.

2. To which school district did the children belong?

From the school registers we were able to find where tuition took place each year from 1847 onwards; from the Church registers we obtained the addresses of the children; and from maps, interviews and fieldwork the exact location of each building. In this way we were able to place the children in their respective school districts, and to measure the distance between home and school on the basis of the site coordinates.

3. Compulsory attendance?

The 1842 law said nothing about a child having to go to school, but instead postulated that every child should be educated. Education, then, could take place either at the school under the guidance of a schoolmaster or in the home under the guidance of the parents. Around 1880, the authorities made school attendance compulsory for six years, beginning at the age of seven. However, we have no indication that the education provided in the home was an effective alternative to proper schooling. In order not to miss any school children, the first age-group selected had to be that of 1830.

68

4. School days in Locknevi

The development of education in a school district can be described in terms of the number of days of schooling offered during the year. The following description is based on information contained in Table 3 and Diagram 22. As we can see, the schooling provided for children varied greatly in length. In the beginning boys were supposed to go to school more often than girls, and for the first five years (1847—51) there were more school days per annum in the permanent primary school in Locknevi than in Ytterbo which the school-master visited for only a couple of months every year.

5. Attendance at school

During the first year of compulsory schooling in Locknevi parish 1847, 123 children attended school for one day or more (see Table 4). In the second year, 1848, 197 children attended. One important reason for this increase was that education was by then provided not only in Locknevi village but also in the district of Ytterbo. From 1849 onwards attendance dropped, despite the fact that the school-master visited each of the four school districts. The latter part of the 1850's witnesses a big decline, but by 1858 a slight improvement was underway.

Table 4 also illustrates the composition of the school population in terms of age; those from 8 to 13 formed the majority.

Attendance at school varied from a minimum of one day to a maximum of all of the days in which schooling was provided (see Diagram 24). Most children attended school for only a few days each year, with the younger children attending more regularly than the older ones and boys attending more regularly than girls.

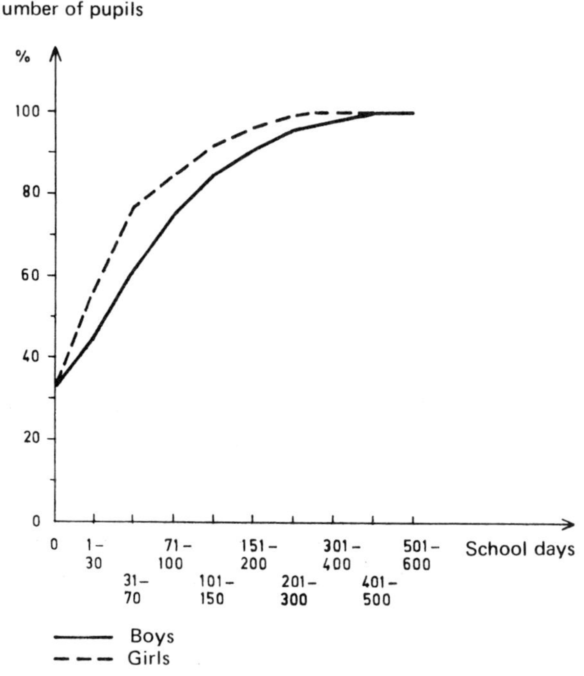

Diagram 22. The total number of days on which boys and girls attended school. Cumulative percentages.

Table 5 illustrates how education gradually became a part of the children's lives. It is only in the last age group that we find all children going to school. One girl was born in 1880 but did not attend school in Locknevi, participated in higher education in the town of Västervik.

The increase in school attendance is depicted in the maps which make up Diagram 23. These illustrate the total number of days on which the children of three different age-horts attended school as well as the occupational status of their parents.

Table 3. Number of school days in Locknevi Parish 1847—1900

<table>
<thead>
<tr><th></th><th colspan="2">Locknevi school district</th><th colspan="2">Vrångfall school district</th><th colspan="2">Ytterbo school district</th><th colspan="2">Toverum school district</th></tr>
<tr><th></th><th>Boys</th><th>Girls</th><th>Boys</th><th>Girls</th><th>Boys</th><th>Girls</th><th>Boys</th><th>Girls</th></tr>
</thead>
<tbody>
<tr><td>1847</td><td>46</td><td>31</td><td></td><td></td><td></td><td></td><td></td><td></td></tr>
<tr><td>1848</td><td>80</td><td>50</td><td></td><td></td><td>28</td><td>24</td><td></td><td></td></tr>
<tr><td>1849</td><td>61</td><td>47</td><td></td><td></td><td>31</td><td>25</td><td></td><td></td></tr>
<tr><td>1850</td><td>60</td><td>34</td><td></td><td></td><td>31</td><td>24[4]</td><td></td><td></td></tr>
<tr><td>1851</td><td>77</td><td>40</td><td></td><td></td><td>29</td><td>19[4]</td><td></td><td></td></tr>
<tr><td>1852</td><td>76</td><td>64</td><td></td><td></td><td>31</td><td>30[4]</td><td colspan="2">26</td></tr>
<tr><td>1853</td><td colspan="2">45</td><td colspan="2">46</td><td colspan="2">32</td><td colspan="2">35</td></tr>
<tr><td>1854</td><td colspan="2">42</td><td colspan="2">50</td><td colspan="2">36</td><td colspan="2">36</td></tr>
<tr><td>1855</td><td colspan="2">39</td><td colspan="2">50</td><td colspan="2">33</td><td colspan="2">41</td></tr>
<tr><td>1856</td><td colspan="2">26</td><td colspan="2">43</td><td colspan="2">33</td><td colspan="2">28</td></tr>
<tr><td>1857</td><td colspan="2">42</td><td colspan="2">44</td><td colspan="2">42</td><td colspan="2"></td></tr>
<tr><td>1858</td><td colspan="2"></td><td colspan="2">39</td><td>45</td><td>44</td><td colspan="2">69</td></tr>
<tr><td>1859</td><td colspan="2">100</td><td>68</td><td>65</td><td colspan="2">76</td><td>55</td><td>54</td></tr>
<tr><td>1860</td><td colspan="2">46</td><td colspan="2">98[1]</td><td colspan="2">106</td><td colspan="2">104</td></tr>
<tr><td>1861</td><td colspan="2">89</td><td colspan="2">108[2]</td><td>98</td><td>100[5]</td><td colspan="2">92</td></tr>
<tr><td>1862</td><td colspan="2">113</td><td colspan="2">103</td><td colspan="2">104</td><td colspan="2">102</td></tr>
<tr><td>1863</td><td colspan="2">102</td><td colspan="2">104[3]</td><td colspan="2">96[6]</td><td colspan="2">110</td></tr>
<tr><td>1864</td><td colspan="2">98</td><td colspan="2">100</td><td colspan="2">96[7]</td><td colspan="2">110</td></tr>
<tr><td>1865</td><td colspan="2">93</td><td colspan="2">50</td><td colspan="2">94[8]</td><td colspan="2">99</td></tr>
<tr><td>1866</td><td colspan="2">94</td><td colspan="2">53</td><td colspan="2">96[4]</td><td colspan="2">96</td></tr>
<tr><td>1867</td><td colspan="2">99</td><td colspan="2">91</td><td colspan="2">96[8]</td><td colspan="2">89</td></tr>
<tr><td>1868</td><td colspan="2">100</td><td colspan="2">94</td><td colspan="2">93[8]</td><td colspan="2">38</td></tr>
<tr><td>1880</td><td colspan="2">48</td><td colspan="2">47</td><td colspan="2">46</td><td colspan="2">43</td></tr>
<tr><td>1890</td><td colspan="2">48</td><td colspan="2">48</td><td colspan="2">96</td><td colspan="2">93</td></tr>
<tr><td>1900</td><td colspan="2">81</td><td colspan="2"></td><td colspan="2">75</td><td colspan="2">84</td></tr>
</tbody>
</table>

[1] Education located to Ranglebo
[2] 58 days education in Grönhult
[3] 46 days education in Dramstorp
[4] Education located to Östantorp
[5] 51 days education in Mantebo
[6] 53 days education in Gunnebo
[7] 44 days education in Gunnebo
[8] Education located to Gunnebo

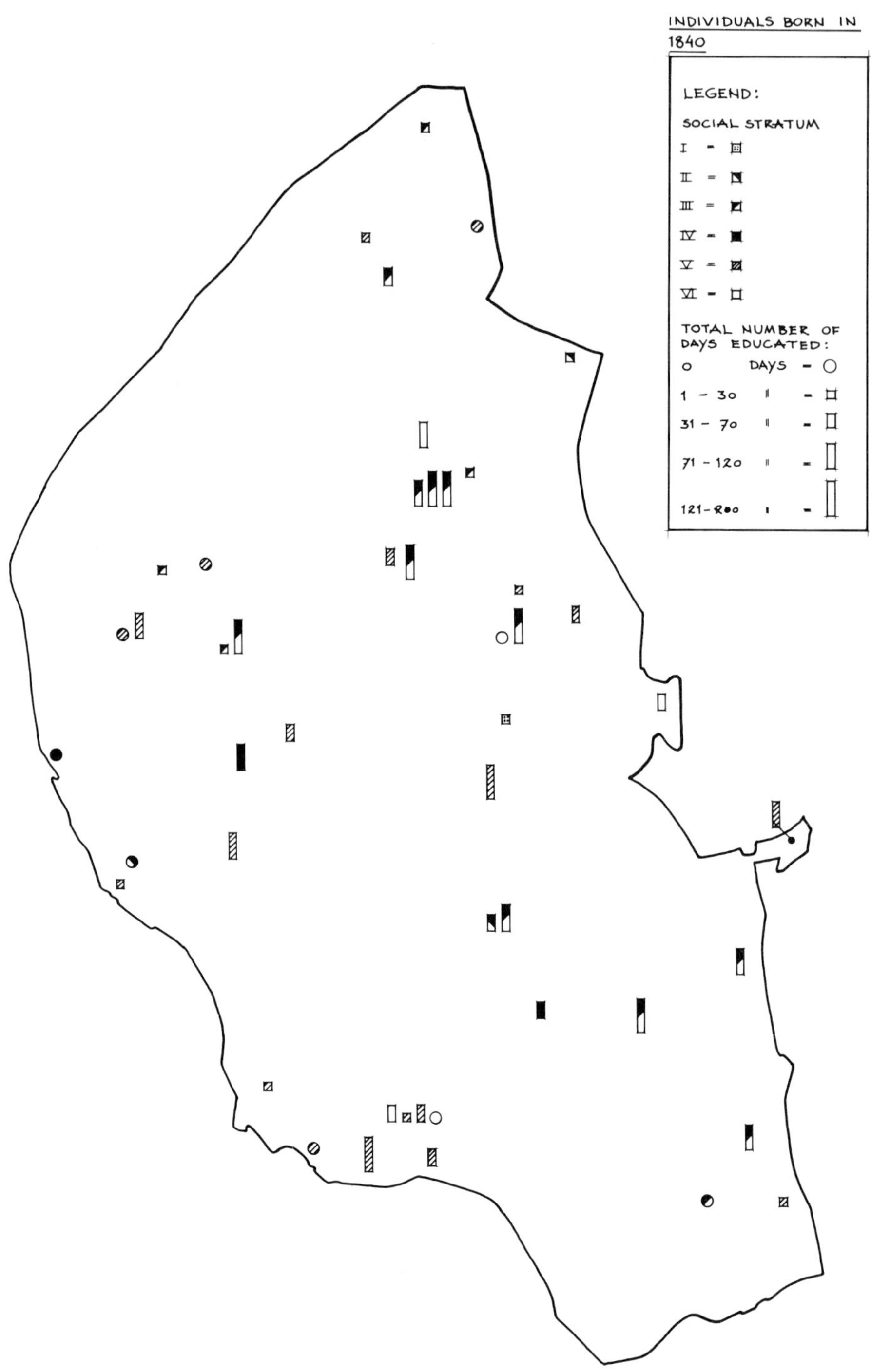

Diagram 23a. Map showing the location of children born in 1840, their social status and the total number of days on which they attended school.

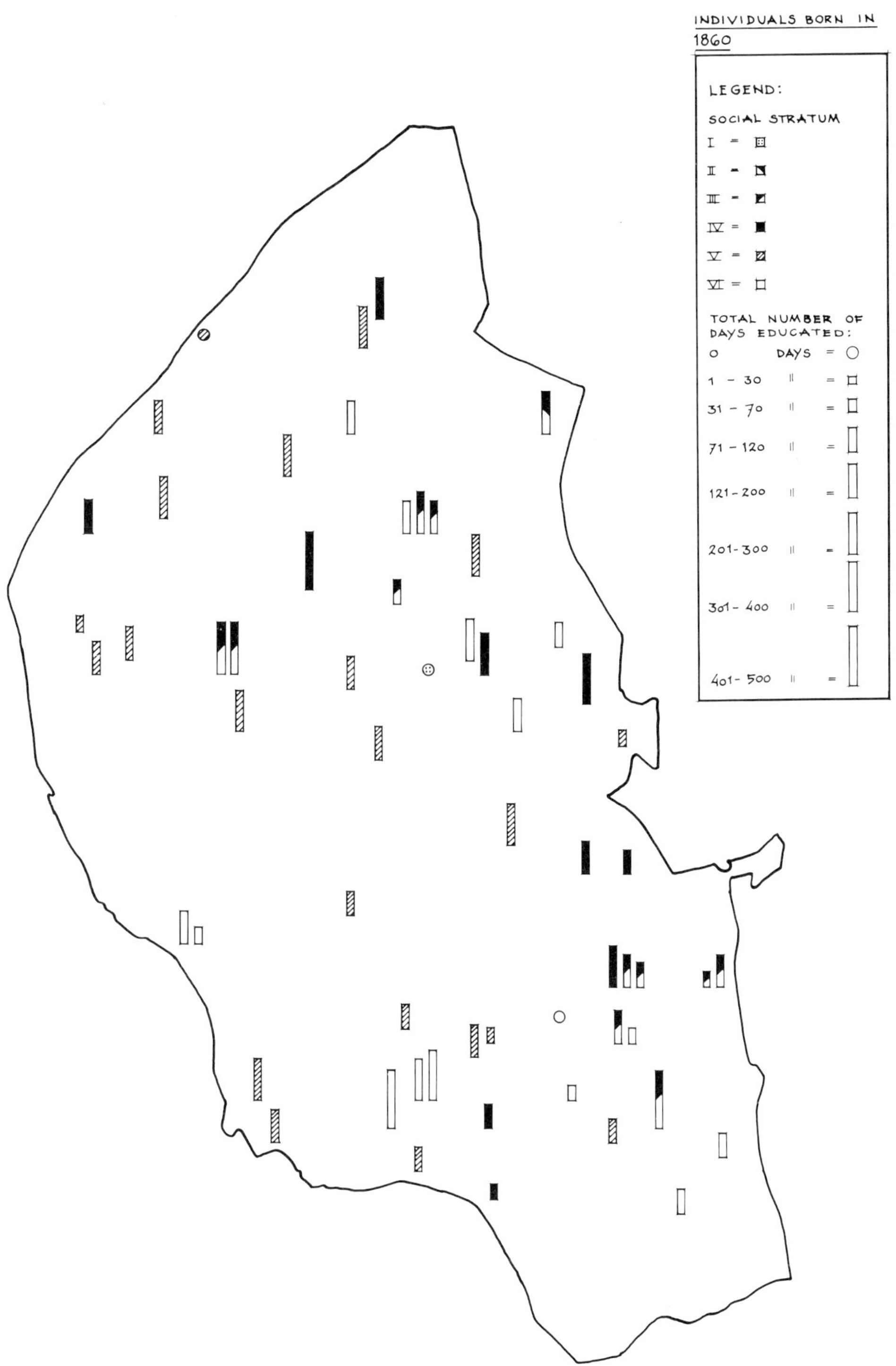

Diagram 23b. Map showing the location of children born in 1860, their social status and the total number of days on which they attended school.

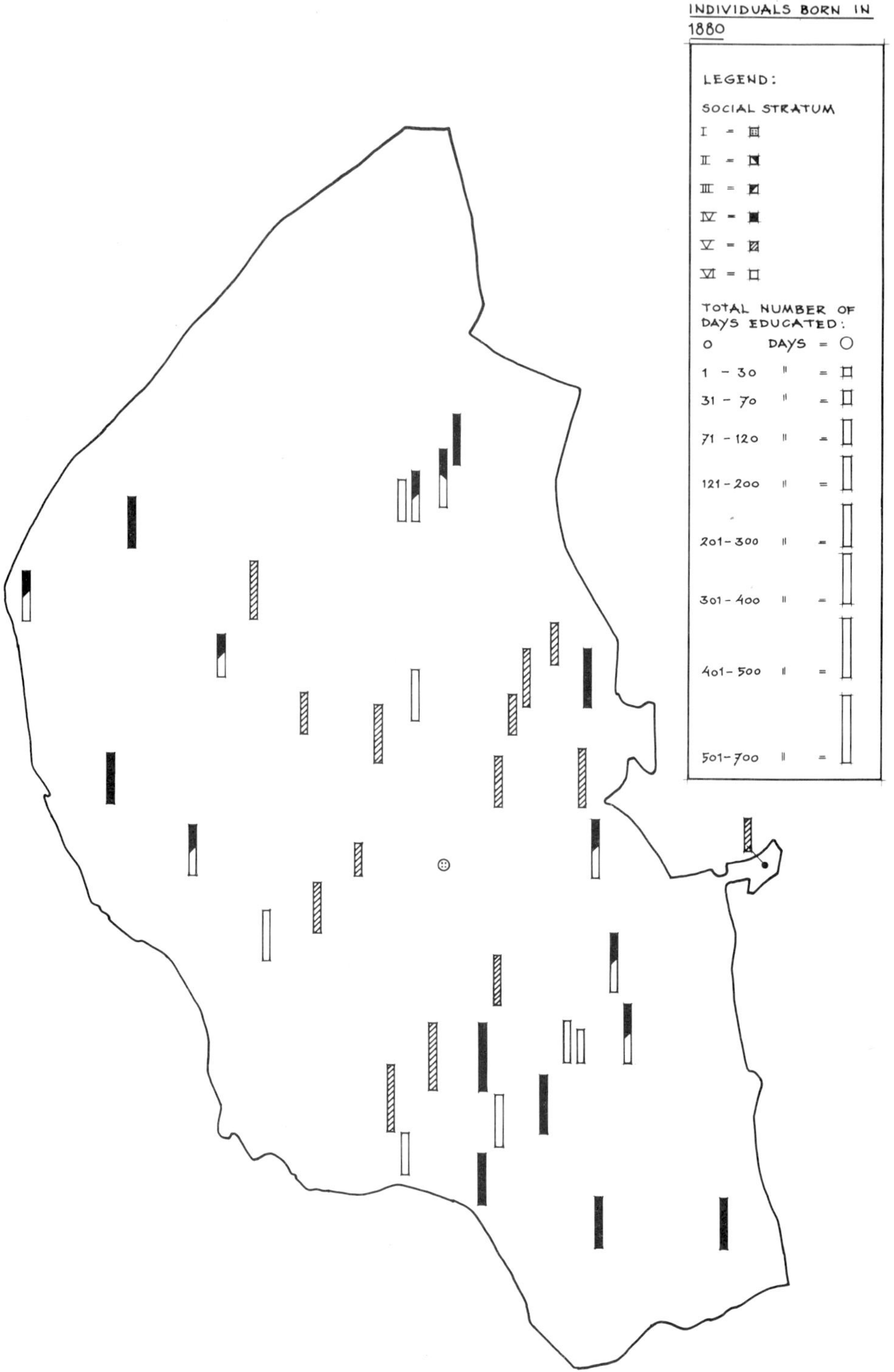

Diagram 23c. Map showing the location of children born in 1880, their social status and the total number of days on which they attended school.

Table 4. School-children distributed after age and education period (year)

Year	Age 5	6	7	8	9	10	11	12	13	14	15	16	17	18	Total
1847	0	3	4	14	11	18	21	13	13	16	7	3	0	0	123
48	0	1	9	18	25	21	31	27	27	21	10	4	3	0	197
49	0	0	4	15	21	22	16	24	18	21	10	0	0	0	151
50	0	3	5	11	24	27	25	22	27	10	3	0	0	0	157
51	0	0	6	22	16	24	25	25	13	16	2	0	2	0	151
52	0	3	5	14	25	20	19	24	22	18	6	3	0	1	150
53	0	1	15	14	14	27	13	15	14	5	2	1	0	0	121
54	0	3	7	23	19	14	23	8	10	7	2	0	0	0	116
55	0	4	15	20	30	18	13	20	4	4	3	0	0	0	131
56	0	1	12	13	14	29	13	8	10	1	0	0	0	0	102
57	0	0	2	8	12	10	13	8	3	2	0	1	0	0	59
58	1	8	5	21	18	22	15	19	4	6	1	0	0	0	120
59	0	2	17	24	32	33	41	23	24	4	1	0	0	0	201
60	0	9	21	33	25	32	31	24	16	14	0	0	0	0	205
61			35	27	35	22	27	32	27	11	3	0	0	0	
62				50	32	40	22	21	28	8	1	0	0	0	
63					55	32	35	17	13	12	2	1	0	0	
64						51	34	27	15	8	2	0	0	0	
65							45	31	18	12	2	1	0	0	
66								47	31	31	8	0	0	0	
67									39	19	11	0	0	0	
68										32	6	0	0	0	
69											1	0	0	0	

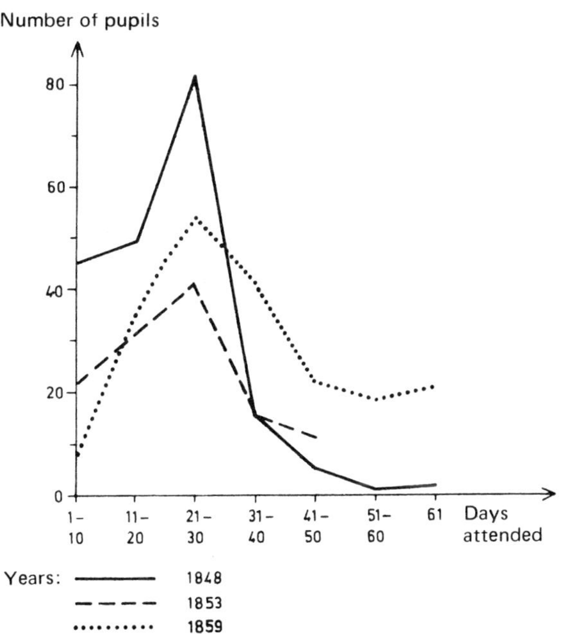

Diagram 24. The distribution of the school children according to school attendance (days/annum)

Table 5. Total number of schooldays per child and during lifetime

Year of birth	Days 0	1– 30	31– 70	71– 100	101– 150	151– 200	201– 300	301– 400	401–
1830	45	0	0	0	0	0	0	0	0
31	40	3	0	0	0	0	0	0	0
32	49	8	0	0	0	0	0	0	0
33	31	17	2	0	0	0	0	0	0
34	22	23	10	0	0	0	0	0	0
35	28	18	14	2	0	0	0	0	0
36	14	21	17	1	0	0	0	0	0
37	23	20	17	6	5	0	0	0	0
38	10	12	11	6	4	0	0	0	0
39	13	10	14	2	10	2	1	0	0
40	13	10	15	9	5	3	0	0	0
41	21	13	7	4	4	4	2	0	0
42	16	7	10	4	3	3	0	0	0
43	15	11	13	10	4	4	1	0	0
44	17	9	8	5	4	1	2	0	0
45	12	8	10	6	3	1	1	0	0
46	15	4	15	15	9	4	4	0	0
47	10	6	14	6	6	3	1	1	0
48	16	10	11	15	11	4	1	1	0
49	12	4	17	11	6	8	5	0	0
50	6	7	6	14	10	4	3	2	0
51	6	7	9	5	10	3	5	1	0
52	5	3	9	7	5	11	14	4	2
53	8	2	7	5	11	6	7	5	4
54	7	3	5	15	11	11	13	7	5
1870	9	1	1	2	1	10	28	13	2
1880	1	0	0	0	0	3	7	16	12

Recruitment to Higher Education 1940–1965

The present high rate of enrolment in institutions of higher education in Sweden is a relatively recent phenomenon. In order to describe recruitment to higher education in Locknevi, we investigated all children born between 1928 and 1949 who were living in Locknevi at the age of 10. By examining school and Church registers, and by interviewing either the former school-children themselves, or their parents, siblings or acquaintances we were able to ascertain their educational attainment. Out of 424 persons we were able to contact 409. Some were dead, a few refused to cooperate and some we could not trace.

The educational attainment of the children of Locknevi in terms of both academic studies and professional training is presented in Table 6. It corresponds closely to the educational status of the Swedish population generally. The table indicates that the education of two-thirds of the children ended after primary school, scarcely 20 per cent reached a secondary level and 4 per cent completed university education. We also find differences between those born in the 1930's and those born in the 1940's; the latter were better educated than the former. In Map 25 we have mapped the locations of all educational institutions at which the children of Locknevi received training after primary school.

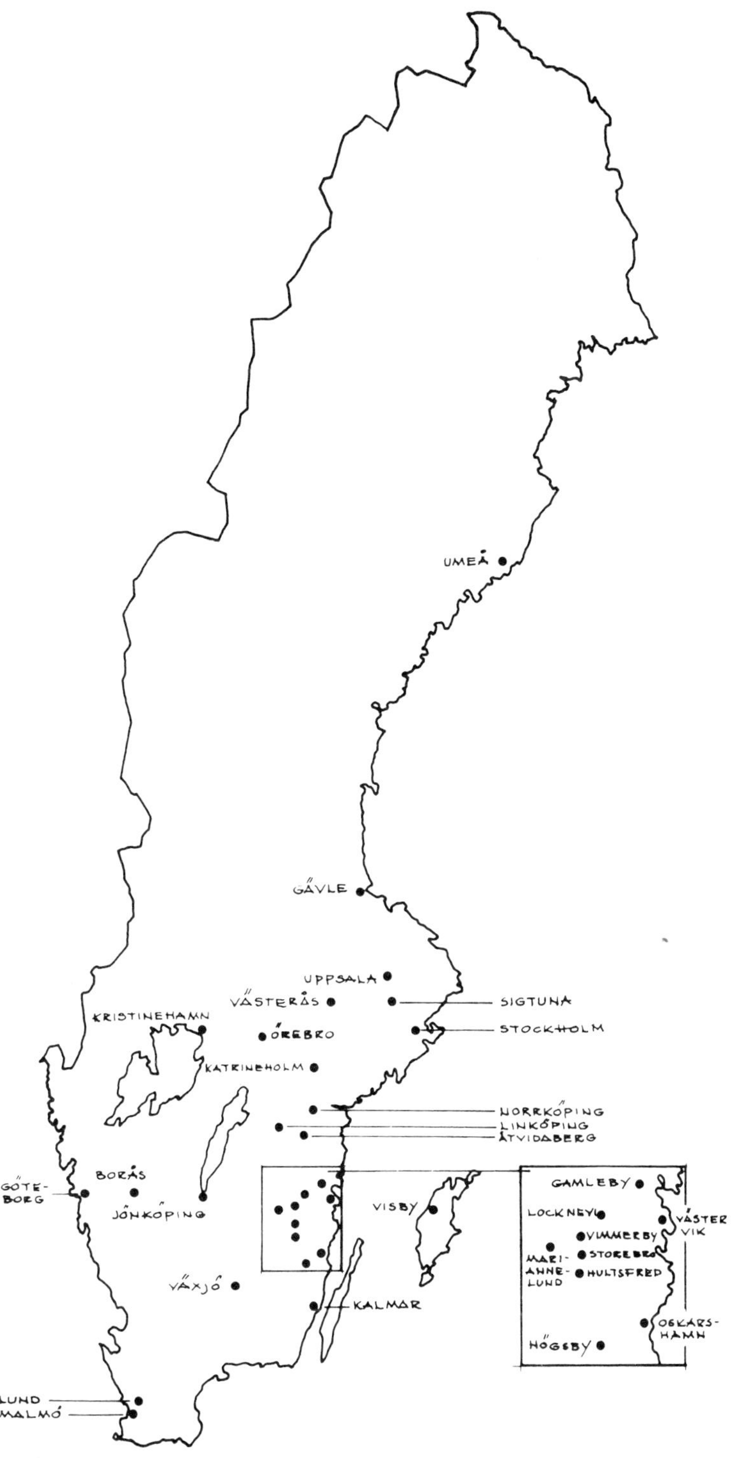

Map 25. Educational institutions at which members of the population received post-primary education.

Table 6. Level of educational attainment of the population

	1928–34	1935–39	1940–44	1945–49	Total
Primary school only	74	76	74	53	277
Secondary school	4	2	3	8	17
People's High School	4	3	4	2	13
Commercial secondary school	1	0	0	1	2
Technical secondary school	0	2	0	0	2
Medical attendant courses	3	2	1	7	13
Industrial secondary school	2	5	8	11	26
Cartographer's courses	0	1	0	0	1
Noncommisioned offers school	0	0	0	1	1
Unspecified, secondary level	1	0	1	2	4
General grammar school	1	0	2	1	4
Technical training school	0	4	0	1	5
Nurses school	3	2	4	3	12
Police school	0	1	0	0	1
Medical secretary courses	0	0	1	0	1
Primary school training college	1	0	0	1	2
Preparatory school training college	0	3	0	0	3
Special teacher's training college	1	1	1	1	4
Apothecary assistants courses	0	0	1	0	1
General university degree	0	0	1	4	5
Grammar school teacher training college	0	0	0	1	1
Social worker training college	0	0	0	1	1
Medical training college	0	0	0	2	2
Dentist training college	0	0	0	1	1
College of technology	0	1	0	1	2
College of commercial science	0	0	0	2	2
Master mariner training college	0	0	0	1	1
Ph. D degree	0	1	0	0	1
Total	95	104	101	105	405

Testing the Hypotheses

Thus far, we have described the educational development of a Swedish parish over two different periods of time. During both periods, major reforms were being carried out in Swedish society as a whole. We have also shown that some families sent their children to primary school in the nineteenth century and some to higher education in the twentieth century while others did not. These differences may be due to differences among families in their knowledge of the newly established school system and its potential benefits, and to their willingness to accept innovations. We shall now proceed to test our hypotheses.

The Role of Information

Today it is difficult, or impossible, for us to know what type of information was transmitted from one person to another in the 19th century. At best we can uncover some of the official decrees recorded in school registers, which at least provide a picture of communication from the authorities to the people. In some cases we can also trace — again through the registers — how people reacted to these decrees.

In 1842, as we have seen, the people of Locknevi were informed that compulsory education was to be introduced in Sweden. Parishes were expected to establish at least one permanent primary school within five years and to engage one trained teacher. Continual discussion took place concerning the location of the first school and the type of building that should be built. All of this discussion, and the eventual building of the school, makes it unlikely that anyone could have been unaware of the existence of the school and the fact that children were supposed to attend it. It is also unlikely that the views held by people concerning the advantages of schooling differed greatly within parishes, although they may have differed from one parish to another. There may also have been differences between the national authorities and the people of Locknevi — in fact, the harsh criticisms of local school authorities made by the school inspectors, who were supposed to oversee school boards and enforce school regulations, bear witness to this. The criticisms in question concerned the buildings, school attendance, the number of teachers employed, the supply of school materials and so forth (see Chapter V).

One of the results of our study indicates that some families were exposed to more pressure from local authorities than others — the children of parents judged to be of low intelligence attended school more regularly than others, for example. Perhaps the authorities felt that these children should attend school because their parents were unable to provide an adequate education in the home.

In the 20th century, we find evidence of pressure from teachers upon parents in order to persuade them to let their more intelligent children continue schooling after reaching the compulsory leaving age. This was related both to the intellectual capacity of the children and to the availibility of non-agrarian occupations outside the limited labour market of Locknevi.

Factors Related to the Acceptance of Innovations

The willingness to accept innovations such as the sending of children to school was investigated in a more formal way. A micro-theory was constructed on the basis of existing knowledge; dependent and independent factors delimited; operational variables defined; and hypotheses formulated and tested.

Diagram 25 sums up the results of the two studies. There is a marked similarity between the factors influencing the pattern of recruitment to compulsory education during the 19th century and to higher education in the 20th century. Family structure, home environment and physical environment were found to be important (see, for instance, Johansson 1972). Socio-economic status was positively related to school attendance, as was a supportive home environment. The distance between home and school was again shown to be significant, in that a long distance had a negative influence upon recruitment.

When we tested our results in a multiple regression model we found quite low degrees of explanation (see Table 7). This was probably due to the fact that we could not include all the factors we knew were important (such as early intelligence and the perceived benefits of education) as the relevant data were unavailable. This lack also limited the choice of operational variables.

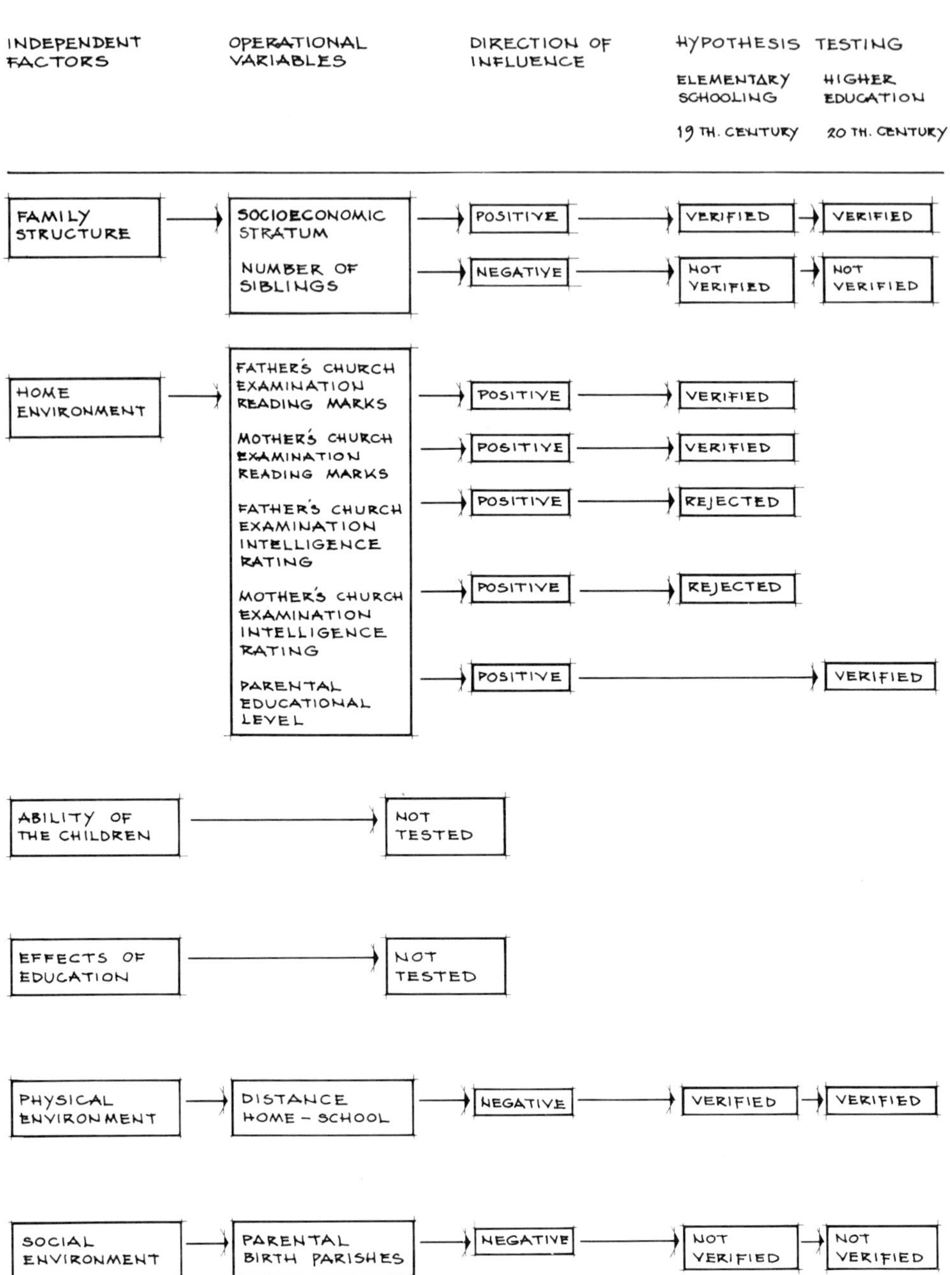

Diagram 25. Summary of the educational recruitment studies.

Table 7. Regression test: Degrees of explanation with the proposed model and with recruitment to elementary education as dependent variable

Year	1930–34	1935–39	1940–44	1945–49
	0,14	0,11	0,16	0,29

Spatial Similarities and Differences within Locknevi Parish

It is of great importance in social studies to include both the physical and social environment among the explanatory factors. Let us give some examples:

Recruitment to primary schools in the 19th century was heavily dependent upon the physical distance between home and school. Living in the periphery of a parish generally implied low school attendance, and this situation was found to be true for the whole of Locknevi.

Recruitment to higher education varied within Locknevi: the school district of Toverum had a lower share of students than Ytterbo, which in turn had lower rates than Locknevi and Vrångfall.

The *quality* of education offered also varied within the parish. Reading ability, for example, was lower in Toverum than in other parts of Locknevi according to the findings of the school inspectors.

An important factor explaining these similarities and differences is the geographic distribution of occupational groups. Hence, while Vrångfall and Ytterbo were always dominated by small-scale farmers, the population of Toverum consisted of people with few resources. Around the village of Locknevi the distribution of different social and occupational groups was fairly even.

The Dimension of Time

We could sum up the above by saying that there was a correlation between some of the factors studied and family decisions concerning the school attendance of children, and that some of these factors varied in strength over time.

Attendance at primary school differed initially according to socio-economic status. As is illustrated in Diagram 26, this relationship gradually decreased in strength, but increased again at the end of the century – a pattern that can be explained by the fact that during the first years of primary schooling in Locknevi school attendance was largely voluntary. This favoured the children of wealthier families, who went to school earlier and more regularly. Dissatisfaction with the slowness of the increase in school attendance led the national authorities to introduce the school inspection system in the early 1860's. Twenty years later their efforts began to bear fruit and attendance became fairly high. The rate of increase was especially high among lower socio-economic groups. By the end of the century, the pressure upon families to send their children to school had decreased, perhaps because of an increasing concern among school inspectors about the quality of education rather than its quantity (see Chapter V). This led to the reappearance of the differences in attendance among socio-economic groups.

The results found when students in higher education were classified to socio-economic groups were rather surprising. Diagram 27 illustrates the recruitment pattern we expected, where children with a high socio-economic background would be consistently over-re-

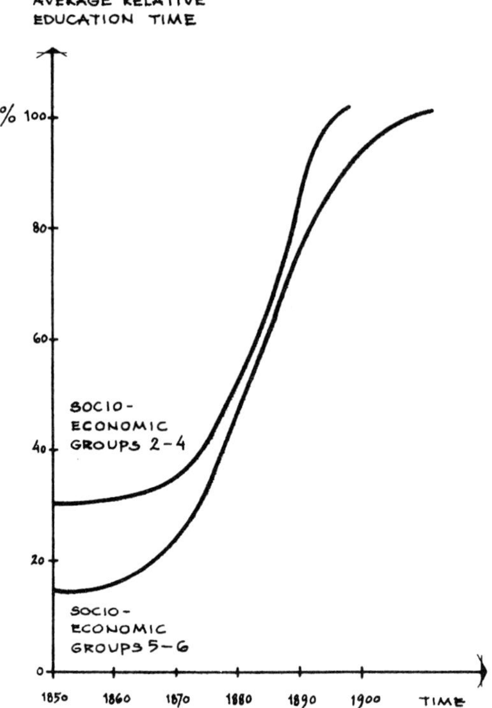

Diagram 26. Attendance at primary school according to socio-economic status.

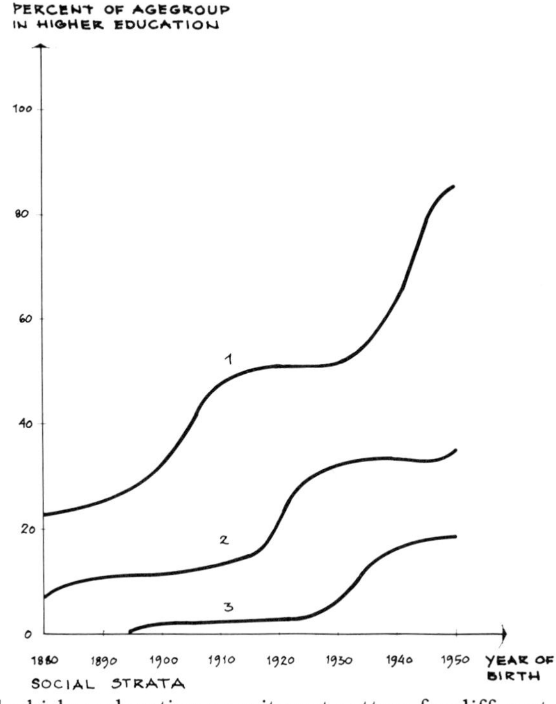

Diagram 27. The higher education recruitment pattern for different strata.

presented compared with lower socio-economic groups. We expected that recruitment would develop in "steps" which corresponded to educational reforms.

As Diagram 28 shows, the recruitment pattern in Locknevi for the highest and lowest occupational groups was as predicted, while recruitment among the middle group (3) was less than expected for the first three age-groups. This was due to the fact that group 3 consisted mainly of owners of small farms. Not until after World War II, when it became clear that a small farm could not possibly support a family, did these consider allowing their children to continue their education after primary school. Previously, at least one child had been expected to take over the farm but, after the large-scale closing down of small farms in the 1950's, most children were released from this obligation.

The Expected Effects of Primary Schooling in Sweden

There are a number of theories concerning the aims of the introduction of compulsory schooling in Sweden. Two of the most common are:

1. That compulsory education was introduced to relieve poverty among lower socio-economic groups in rural areas.

2. That compulsory education was introduced to provide a means for social control.

Both of these theories assume that the poorest people in society were reached by the schools. However, findings show that the proletariat, which has a high rate of mobility between different parishes, actually had little contact with the educational system. Hence, neither of the two aims mentioned above could have been achieved — at least not in the parish of Locknevi.

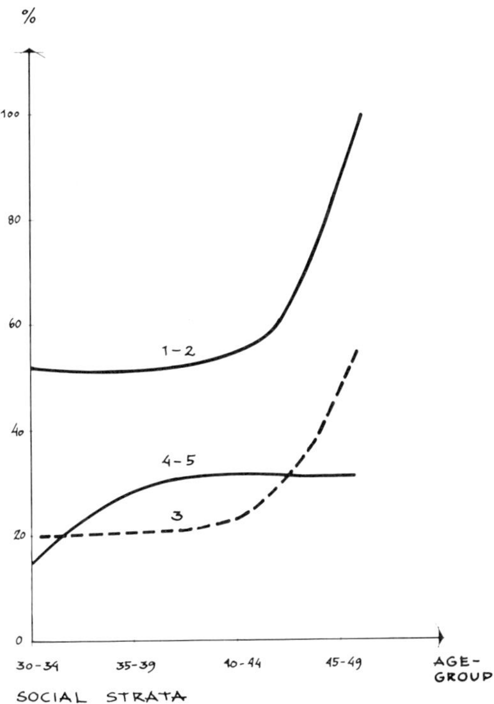

Diagram 28. Recruitment pattern to higher education between different age groups and social strata.

VII. THE SPATIAL AND SOCIAL CONSEQUENCES OF EDUCATION: TWO LONGITUDINAL STUDIES

A. The Problem

During the past 150 years, three major educational reforms have been carried out in Sweden. The first reform in 1842–47, as has already been noted, involved the establishment of a six-year elementary school in every parish and the introduction of "compulsory" attendance for every child of school age (7–13 years). The second form consisted of the expansion of voluntary, higher education during the 1940's and 1950's, while the third concerned the reorganization of the elementary school. The latter began in 1957.

One question that a human geographer should ask in relation to this development is: What effects have the school reforms had upon both the individual and society? As geographers are especially interested in spatial processes, an important question for us in relation to school reforms is whether or not these reforms influenced the spatial location of people.

A closely related question concerns social mobility. A change in spatial position (spatial mobility) often implies a change in the amount of resources available or *vice versa*. A more general issue is whether education affects the social and also spatial mobility of people and, thereby, the spatial structure of society (see Chapter I).

In two studies carried out by Hoppe (1977 and 1978a) the following questions were investigated: Did the elementary school reforms and the expansion of voluntary higher education change the social and spatial structure of Sweden? Implicit in this question was the further question of whether the reforms also changed the pattern of social and spatial mobility.

B. Aim of the Studies

In addition to the general aim described above, the two studies each had a more specific aim. The aim of the first was to examine the effects of the expansion of education during the latter half of the 19th century upon the life-paths of six age-cohorts in Locknevi parish, and to see whether there were any differences *between* or *within* the six cohorts in relation to educational achievement. A life-path was here defined as the registered spatial and social positions occupied by an individual from the age of ten to the age of forty. The dimension of *real competence* (see below) was considered to be important here.

The aim of the second study was to *describe* and to *analyse* the differences among the life-paths of a test population born between 1928 and 1949 and who were living in Locknevi parish at the age of ten. An attempt was also made to *explain* why such differences developed between different age-groups and between different individuals in one or several age-groups. The dimension of *formal competence* was regarded as more important here.

The two dimensions of competence which result from education, real and formal competence, require further explanation. Real competence consists of the knowledge, skill and understanding acquired by the individual through education. The same level of education (elementary etc.) may result in different levels of real competence in different individuals, depending upon their receiving ability and their intelligence, for example. Formal competence, on the other hand, is the competence acquired through the completion of different educational levels (educational attainment). An individual has a formal competence on the elementary level, the secondary level, the university undergraduate level etc. The higher levels of formal competence also tend to tie people to certain professions or branches of professions (this effect will in future be termed 'sectorial barring').

The real competence dimension was studied using a test population whose formal competence was low, usually a measure of elementary education. Hence there were no great formal competence differences "disturbing" the analysis. The formal competence dimension, on the other hand, was studied using a test population which had quite large differences in educational attainment. However, this means that there were also differences between individuals in terms of real competence and, as the two dimensions tend to co-vary, there was some difficulty in deciding which dimension was the more important.

C. Background to the Studies

As the aim of the research outlined above was rather complex, it was necessary to use a rather complex model. It is not possible to explain the development of individual life-paths by concentrating only upon formal competence and real competence. Instead, it is necessary to use complete individual life-biographies, where educational background in the broad sense is related to education and life-path development.

It is difficult to find previous research dealing with all the dimensions included in the above discussions. Studies have focused upon social development, educational development in relation to family background, spatial development in relation to educational attainment and so forth. Consequently, an inductive theory was formulated on the basis of the framework in Diagram 29 and earlier, partial, findings were placed in this context.

Clearly, longitudinal individual studies were necessary if the general aim was to be fulfilled. Previous longitudinal studies which include spatial dimensions are few and far between; most of them have studied only one or two age-cohorts selected from various places. As a result, societal change is "kept constant" inside the study, despite the fact that it is changes in the society that ought to be explained. When using several different age-cohorts or age-groups, two aspects of development should be considered: individual life-path development and societal development over time.

Diagram 29. Main theoretical concepts.

D. Formulating a Micro-Theory. 1.

Educational background, educational recruitment and educational achievement.

A number of investigations have shown that recruitment to higher education in Sweden is socio-economically askew: children of high socio-economic standing are over-represented among those in gymnasium education (see for example Gesser 1976; Fägerlind 1975; Dahn 1936), and among those in post-gymnasial education. The results presented in Chapter VI show that this has also been the situation in Locknevi at various times during this century. Of course this is not unique — selective recruitment to higher education occurs in many other countries such as the USA (see Jencks 1972; Hauser and Featherman 1977 etc.) and France (see Boudon 1973; Bourdieu 1976). These studies also show that parental educational attainment and home environment are very important factors in determining the pattern of recruitment to higher education.

Geographers such as Pålsson (1958) and Holm and Häggström (1972) have shown that the pattern of recruitment is also biased spatially. In any given area (e.g. a gymnasial 'umland' or a university region) students living close to the educational unit are over-represented in relation to students from the outer limits of the area. The upper socio-economic strata are less distance sensitive; more such children go on to higher education despite the fact that they may live far from the educational unit. Spatial position is thus also a resource — if one's home is close to the school, it is less expensive to acquire some education.

These findings refer to recruitment to voluntary higher education. Educational a-chievement (step 2 in the theoretical framework) is also related to the factors outlined above, but is more strongly related to home environment and individual intelligence. As intelligence is largely a product of the same factors as educational achievement (see Bloom 1964) there is some multi-collinearity between them. In the present research, the intelligence dimension was not investigated further as the background factors were considered more important and more relevant to the aims set out earlier.

As we have already seen, participation in elementary schooling during the establishment phase, as well as achievement measured in the form of school marks and Church examination register marks, may also be related to the educational background factors previously mentioned. In a study of early elementary education in Bygdeå parish in northern Sweden, Johansson (1972) found that school participation was related to socio-economic status, distance from school and the vicar's catechism rating of parental intelligence. The latter can be taken as a rough measure of parental educational status or attainment. School grades were related to the length of time children had been registered in school and to the socio-economic status of the parents. These results accord well with the findings from Locknevi presented in Chapter VI on recruitment to elementary education.

The results from Bygdeå are also quite similar to the results found in previous studies of recruitment of voluntary educations described earlier in this section. Educational background factors seem to exert a similar influence on recruitment to both voluntary higher education and achievement in compulsory elementary education. Hence, the same background factors have been included in the micro-theory to be tested on the 19th century population (the real competence dimension) and on the 20th century population (the formal competence dimension).

We can now sum up some important factors concerning both educational achievement on the elementary level and recruitment to voluntary higher education.

A. Elementary educational achievement and recruitment to higher education are related to educational background, especially socio-economic resources and home environment.

B. The spatial position of the home in relation to the school affects both elementary school achievement and recruitment to higher education.

C. Recruitment to higher education is dependent upon achievement at the previous educational level.

These relationships make up the first stage of the micro-theory (see Diagram 30). As this theory is to be tested on two different populations, using two different dimensions of education and two different source sets, *two* operational versions of the micro-theory are necessary. In the first version, tested on the six age-cohorts born in 1830, 1840, 1850, 1860, 1870 and 1880, school achievement on the elementary level (i.e. real competence) was the educational dimension used and measured. In the second version, tested on four age-groups born between 1928 and 1949, the educational level attained (i.e. formal competence) was utilized. Intelligence was seen as a factor which affects both recruitment and achievement, but which is itself a product of educational background and biological heritage. It has not been possible to evaluate any specific intelligence measure in the operational models but, as Fägerlind (1975) among others has shown, intelligence ratings after a few years of schooling tend to correlate strongly with school grades. The latter can thus be used as a rough measure of intelligence as well as of school achievement.

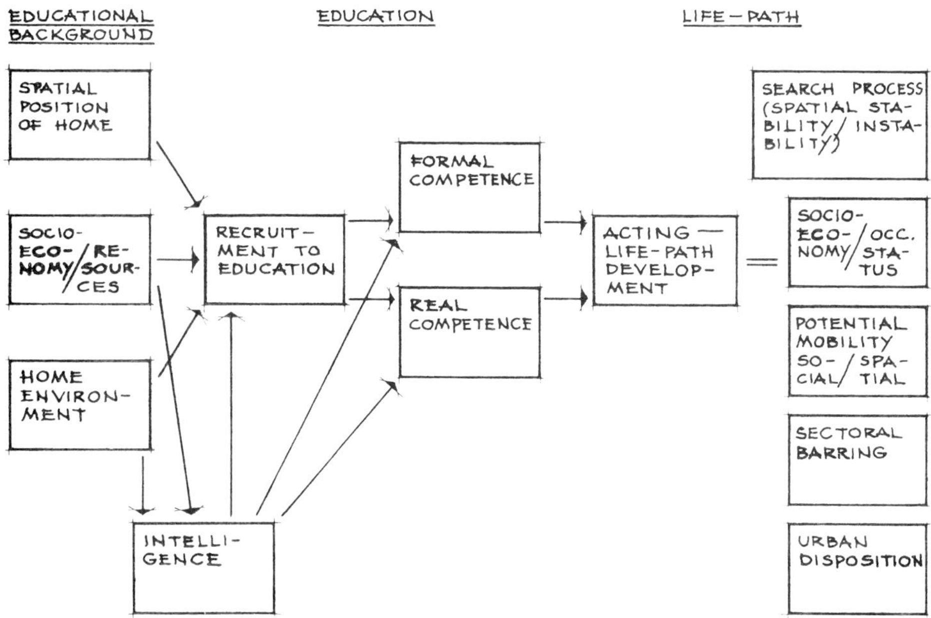

Diagram 30. Schematic outline of the utilized micro-theory.

E. Formulating a Micro–Theory. 2.

Educational achievement and life-path development

The life-path has two *main* dimensions, one social and one spatial. Husén et al. (1969) found a strong relationship between educational attainment and eventual socio-economic status. Fägerlind (1975) has shown that, as recruitment to education is socially askew, the *real* relationship is between social background and life-path socio-economic achievement. These results verify the Coleman resource conversion theory (see Coleman 1971) which argues that educational background resources are converted into educational achievement which is in turn converted into socio-economic status. This is not a *direct* resource transfer but an *indirect* one and it is probably typical of industrial and post-industrial societies, where direct livelihood position transfer is becoming less common. Similar results have been found in many other countries such as France (Boudon 1973), the USA (Hauser and Featherman 1977) and Northern Ireland (Boyle 1977). Consequently, the socio-economic dimension in the second stage of the micro-theory (see Diagram 30) was formulated in relation to educational achievement, but, as educational achievement is in turn related to social background, education was seen as a resource converter between social background and life-path development.

In the past, the spatial effects of education on the individual level have generally been studied in two ways. The first is the general migration study (see, for example Gerger 1968 and Hamilton 1959) where the *move* is the object of study and where movements of the same individual might be counted one or several times, depending upon where measurement takes place (usually at an administrative boundary) and on the individual's spatial behaviour. Non-movers have of course not been included. Variables such as educational status and socio-economic status or income have normally been measured for each movement, as well as changes brought about by the move. The results of such studies are unanimous: the higher an individual's education, the more frequently and the longer he moves. Many investigations of this kind have concentrated upon inter-regional migration but, as most spatial mobility is intra-regional (see Hägerstrand 1957), there is not necessarily the same relationship between all spatial mobility and the background variables discussed here.

The other way to study individual migration is to use the longitudinal approach. As this is much more complicated, in terms of both data collection and data processing, only a small number of such studies have been carried out. Neymark (1961) found in his ten year follow-up study of a sample from one Swedish age-cohort that there were significant differences between different educational attainment groups: people with elementary education only were far more immobile in space than those with higher education. In rural-urban terms, Neymark found that migrants to towns were better educated than non-migrants who remained in the countryside. He also found that the relationship was weaker when only intra-regional rural-urban migration was analyzed. Hence, *local* rural-urban migration was less dominated by an educational élite.

In longitudinal studies of 19th century age-cohorts, Carlsson (1977) and Martinius (1977) found that the non-propertied strata were *more* spatially mobile than the propertied. As socio-economic status (see above) is usually correlated with educational status, the findings of Carlsson and Martinius are somewhat contrary to those of Neymark.

Rundblad (1964) found that "geographical" moves occurred mainly among the better-educated but that moves between different places of work within a specific town or urban area were more frequent among the less well-educated, among people originally from rural areas and among people of low socio-economic status. Similar results have been reported for several developing countries, such as Sierra Leone (Riddell 1970), Ghana (Caldwell 1969) and Chile (Herrick 1965)

The spatial dimension of the second stage of the micro theory can be expressed as in Diagram 30. There is probably a strong interaction between the social and spatial dimensions; educational achievement can lead to higher socio-economic status but only if the educated person is able to move to, or create, appropriate positions.

F. The Operational Model. A: The 1830—1880 Population

It is probably not possible to test a theory or model without any operationalization and formulation of relevant variables. The variables and the operational hypotheses used in the present two studies are discussed in different sections (VII:F and G). The reason for this partition is twofold: i) the sources utilized in the studies were quite different and requires different approaches and ii) the two educational dimensions require different measures.

For the first population studied (that of 1830—1880), the micro-theory consisted of three different factor complexes comprising educational background: the spatial position of the home, the socio-economic resources available and the home environment. Home location was quite easy to determine, as all dwellings in Locknevi from 1800 until 1977 were located and measured with site co-ordinates within the present project (see Fogelvik and Hoppe 1976). Using a similar method to determine the location of schools, we can obtain the distance between the home and school through a simple calculation. The distance is as the crow flies, as it was not considered feasible to reconstruct paths, winter roads over the lakes and so on in order to give a more exact measure — such detail was not needed anyway. The second factor complex, socio-economic resources, was far more difficult to operationalize in its entirety. Ideally, this should consist of a component index including income after tax, social status, property owned and occupational position. Unfortunately, it has not yet been possible for us nor anyone else (see for example Lundsjö 1975) to construct such an index with the available sources; instead, an occupational status scheme with six different social groups or strata was used (see Appendix 1). To simplify the task of deciding when changes had taken place, it was essential to include quite a lot of groups in the scheme — or in other words, to have a fine-meshed net. However, if changes in the nomenclature of the sources or any other "false" changes take place, the individual socio-economic change will also be false. To avoid such false changes, a wide-meshed occupational group scheme should be used. The classification scheme used here represents a compromise between these two positions.

The third factor complex, home environment, was measured by several operational variables. One was socio-economic resources, which has already been described; a second the number of siblings registered, and parental family status a third. The final home environment measure utilized was parental interest, measured using Church examination marks for reading and intelligence. All of the educational background variables were measured when the children studied were 10 years of age.

The measures of educational achievement also comprised a number of variables. The first educational measure consisted of the ratio between the number of days a child was present at school and the total number of days on which schooling was offered. The second was the school grades for subjects which were taught *after* the children had learnt to read (writing, mathematics, history, geography and religion). An index variable called "relative knowledge" was constructed using the grades for these subjects, summed and related to the mean of the respective age-cohorts. In order to obtain a check on the school achievement scores, the reading marks for the children were collected from both school registers and Church examination registers, and standardized into the final two educational achievement variables.

Life-path development was expressed operationally in two ways. Firstly, continuous observations of the relevant variables from the ages of ten to forty allow us to illustrate the life-path through different types of *trajectories*. Secondly, two different *cross-sections* through these life-paths, at twenty-five and forty years, enable us to compare individuals within the same age-cohort and between different cohorts. According to the micro-theory, life-path development consists of two major dimensions and five main factors. Of these, only four are to be used and operationalized in this first theory test because the fifth life-path factor, sectoral barring, should only occur among people with a high formal competence.

Several individual variables were used in the study to illustrate these four factors, and were measured as follows: the different parishes in which an individual lived were described in terms of site co-ordinates and position in an urban hierarchy (rural, minor urban, etc.). Socio-economic position at various times were determined using the same scheme as for parental status determination.

The number of migratory moves inside and outside parishes were also counted as well as the physical distances from the starting-point. With these measures, we were able to test a few operational hypotheses derived from the micro-theory. These were:

1. Educational achievement is heavily dependent upon educational background.

2. Life-path development as specified in the sub-hypotheses below is dependent upon educational achievement and thus also upon educational background.

A. High educational achievement (high real competence) results in an urban disposition and high potential mobility, expressed in high real mobility.
B. High educational achievement results in an increased tendency to emigrate (derived from A).
C. High educational achievement leads to high socio-economic status.
D. High educational achievement renders the spatial search process more effective and thus results in fewer short, circular and static migrations.

These hypotheses are tested in Chapter VIII:B. The sources used were Church examination registers for all the parishes that the population had moved into as well as the migration registers of these parishes. For an evaluation of the sources see Fogelvik, Gerger and Hoppe (1980). Real competence was measured using school marks from the school registers of Locknevi; this was discussed in Chapter VI. For those few persons who had gone beyond elementary school, educational attainment was quantified using gymnasium catalogues from the actual schools.

G. The operational model. B: The 1928—1949 population

The educational background of the second population was operationalized in terms of six variables. The socio-economic resources factor was measured using an occupational level scheme (see Appendix 2), somewhat different from the one used in the earlier investigation. In order to acquire a diversified measure, a horizontal grouping identical with the one used for classifying jobs in recent Swedish censuses was also used. Home environment was quantified using the variables number of siblings as well as parental educational attainment as a measure of their interest in the children's schooling. Finally, a simple school district variable was used to yield a spatial measure of the home location. As the gymnasiums, professional schools etc. open to the children of Locknevi were all located at quite a distance from the parish, the spatial position of the home *within* the parish was considered to be of minor importance.

The formal competence acquired was expressed in terms of two variables, competence level and competence field. The competence field variable cannot, of course, be used in any statistical analysis but is a means for measuring sectoral barring.

Life-paths were again quantified in two ways, one longitudinal and one cross-sectional. The variables were exactly the same as in the previous study: socio-economic level, location of the home parish in an urban hierarchy, site co-ordinates etc.

The operational hypotheses derived from the micro-theory and tested here were:

1. A "good" educational background yields high formal competence.

2. A. High formal competence results in an urban disposition.
   B. High formal competence leads to high socio-economic status.
   C. High formal competence results in an effective spatial search process characterized by long-distance migrations with little static or circular movement.
   D. High formal competence leads to sectoral barring, where those educated in one field are unwilling to change from this field during their working lives.
   This also leads to a pattern of long-distance migrations, as qualified positions are scarce and are available only in the larger cities.

The sources used in this second study and theory test differ somewhat from those used earlier. The life-path measures were obtained from interviews with the population involved and with their families, and the educational measures were obtained in the same way. In only a few cases were controls against written sources needed. The educational background variables, however, were collected from school registers and from the population registers of Locknevi.

In Chapter VIII:C, the results of the hypotheses testing are presented.

VIII. TESTING THE PROPOSED LONGITUDINAL MODELS

A. Real competence: Educational Background and Educational Achievement

Before going on to the more formal testing of the hypotheses proposed, the home background of the 19th century population studied should be examined (see Tables 8–12). As we can see, about 40 per cent of the population consisted of landed children while 60 per cent belonged to the landless class. The number of siblings was higher among the landed than the landless, which supports the description given in Chapter II. The other home environment variable, the Church examination register marks of the parents, is illustrated in Tables 10–11. There was only a small amount of variance between people, and a fairly weak correlation between socio-economic status and Church register marks (around 0.2 for the entire population, somewhat higher for the earlier age-cohorts). Most parents had ratings of fair (code 6) for reading and acceptable (code 4) for intelligence, giving a mean mark of 5.

To give some idea of the spatial mobility of the population (or rather that of the parental generation) between the time of birth and ten years of age, the parishes of origin are described in Table 12, 286 out of 303 persons were born inside the local area, within a radius of 20 kilometers from Locknevi. Only three persons were born outside the region delimited in Map 26, approximately 40 kilometers from Locknevi or more. We can conclude that if any mobility took place it was largely circular and that people moved for short distances only, perhaps just from one hamlet to another.

The spatial distribution of the homes of the members of three age-cohorts at the age of ten is given in Maps 27–29. The socio-economic status of these cohorts is also illustrated. There were no marked differences between landed and landless children in relation to the distance between home and school for the parish as a whole but, inside the single village there were clear home location differences (see for example the Locknevi estate maps of Chapter III).

Table 13 illustrates the total number of days of school attended for the whole population. Children born in 1830 did not go to school at all, while all children born in 1880 attended school for at least 150 days during their childhood. Seven children out of the original 303 attended higher education in some form, two out of these seven completed gymnasium and one of the two studied at university. Higher education was undertaken in Västervik, some 50 kilometers away and university studies were available in Lund or Uppsala. Sixtyseven children did not attend school at all (see Table 14). The mean value of the relative knowledge variable (see Section VII:F) for each co-hort steadily increases, as can be seen in Table 15.

The testing of the first step of the model was done with a series of multiple regressions, testing educational background against relative knowledge, relative number of schooldays and the two types of reading marks. These results are summarized in Table 16. As we can see, educational background accounted for between 18 and 25 per cent of the variance in reading achievement. Educational background finally accounted for 24 to 50 per cent of the variance of the relative knowledge variable. The first part of the proposed model was thus supported, especially in relation to the relative knowledge measure of real competence. The introduction of the elementary school favoured those from homes which were better off in terms of both socio-economic status and spatial position.

Table 8. Socio-economic status for the population at 10 years of age (Classification in Appendix 1)

Cohort	Socio-economic stratum						Total
	1	2	3	4	5	6	
1830	0	3	11	4	17	11	46
1840	1	3	16	3	20	5	48
1850	1	3	6	6	20	7	43
1860	1	1	10	10	23	13	60
1870	3	1	9	12	28	14	67
1880	1	1	7	9	14	7	39
Total	7	12	59	44	122	59	303

Table 9. Average numbers of siblings of the different strata and birth-age cohorts

Cohort	Stratum (1–4 = landed, 5–6 = landless)						Total number of individuals in each cohort
	1	2	3	4	5	6	
1830	—	4.0	3.2	4.3	5.5	2.9	46
1840	7.0	4.7	3.1	4.3	3.8	3.0	48
1850	2.0	2.7	3.8	3.0	2.6	2.0	43
1860	3.0	3.0	3.4	3.4	2.7	3.3	60
1870	3.8	1.0	3.6	4.5	3.3	1.9	67
1880	8.0	1.0	3.4	2.8	3.7	1.7	39
Total	7	12	59	44	122	59	303

Table 10. Fathers' catechization register marks (reading + intelligence/2)

Cohort	Mean mark							Number of individuals
	2	3	4	5	6	7	8	
1830	0	0	6	32	3	0	0	41
1840	0	1	6	37	0	1	0	45
1850	0	1	5	34	0	0	1	41
1860	0	0	7	41	7	0	1	56
1870	0	1	8	35	14	3	0	61
1880	2	5	7	12	8	2	0	36
Total	2	8	39	190	32	6	2	280

92

Table 11. Mother's catechization register marks (reading + intelligence/2)

Cohort	Mean mark							Number of individuals
	2	3	4	5	6	7	8	
1830	0	1	5	32	1	0	0	39
1840	0	0	7	40	0	1	0	48
1850	0	1	4	32	0	0	1	38
1860	0	1	6	38	9	1	1	56
1870	0	1	8	36	15	4	0	64
1880	0	3	9	16	7	4	0	39
Total	0	7	39	194	32	10	2	284
							Loss	19

Table 12. The birth-parishes of the studied cohort members. For a definition of local area and region, see Map 26.

Parish of birth	Birth-age cohort						Total
	1830	1840	1850	1860	1870	1880	
Locknevi	42	30	36	46	53	31	238
Vimmerby	0	0	1	1	0	0	2
Frödinge	1	4	0	0	0	1	6
Djursdala	0	1	0	1	1	0	3
Södra Vi	0	1	0	1	1	1	4
Tuna	0	0	2	0	0	0	2
Hallingeberg	1	2	1	2	0	2	8
Odensvi	0	0	1	0	2	1	4
Hjorted	0	2	1	1	2	0	6
Blackstad	0	3	0	3	4	0	10
Hycklinge	1	1	0	1	0	0	3
Total, Local area	45	44	42	56	63	36	286
Målilla	0	1	1	0	0	0	2
Vena	0	0	0	1	2	1	4
Döderhult	0	1	0	0	1	0	2
Västervik	0	0	0	2	0	0	2
Törnsfall	1	0	0	0	0	0	1
Gladhammar	0	1	0	1	0	0	2
Dalhem	0	0	0	0	0	1	1
Total, region	1	3	1	4	3	2	14
Stockholm						1	
Högsby		1					
Västerås					1		
						Total	303

Map 26. Region – Local area (Region delimited by map).

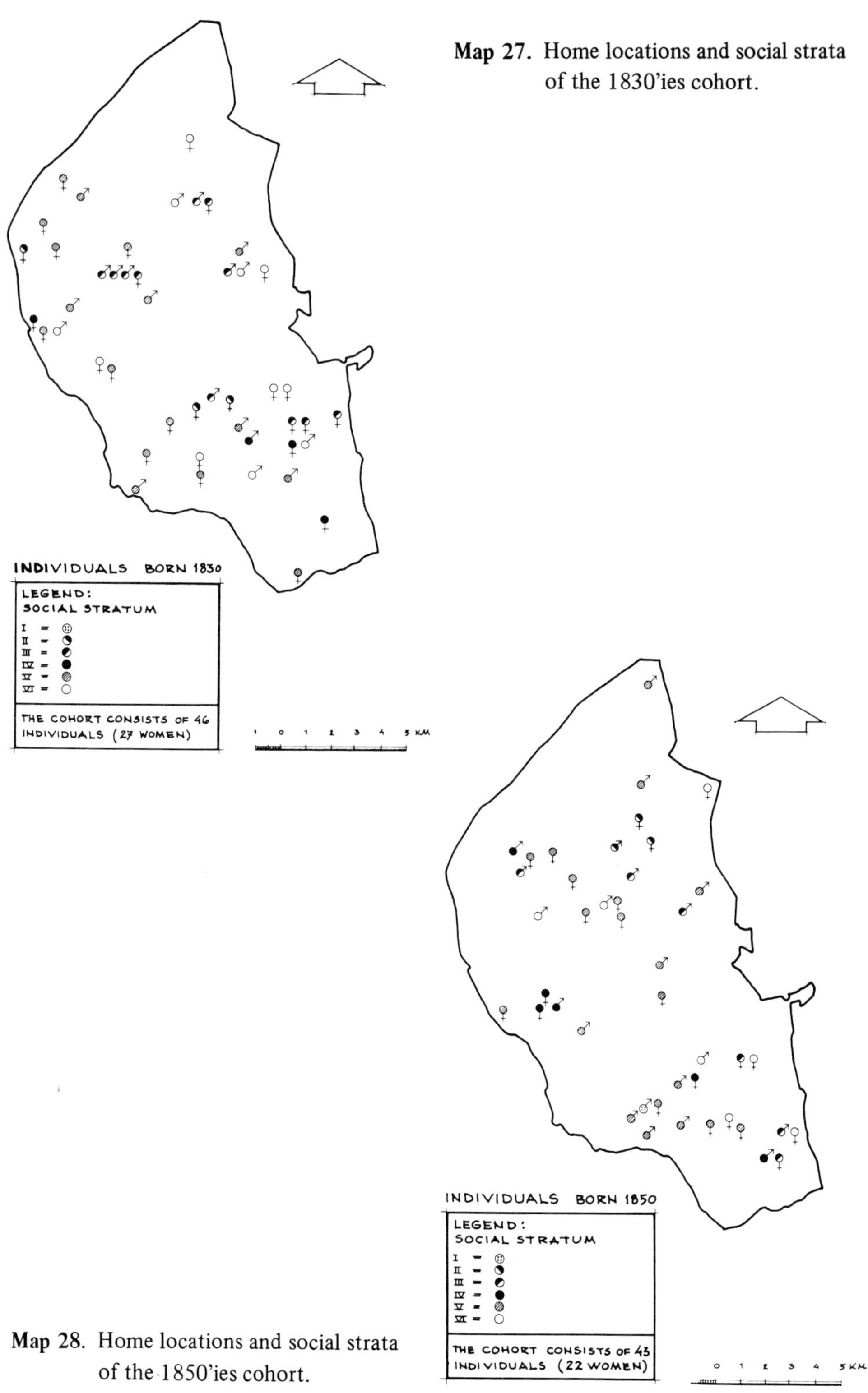

Map 27. Home locations and social strata of the 1830'ies cohort.

Map 28. Home locations and social strata of the 1850'ies cohort.

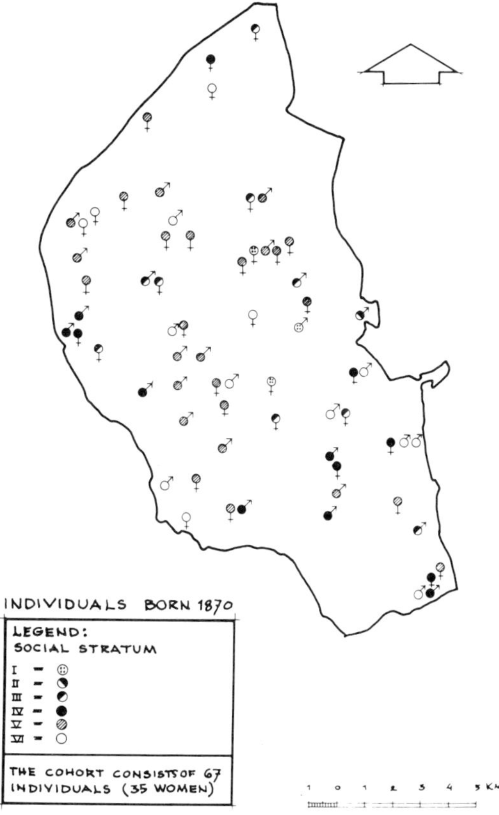

Map 29. Home locations and social strata of the 1870'ies cohort.

Table 13. Total number of schooldays for the studied age cohorts over their lifetimes.

	Total number of schooldays									Total number of individuals
	0	1–30	31–70	71–100	101–150	151–200	201–300	301–400	401–500	500–	
1830	46										46
1840	9	11	10	8	5	4					47
1850	3	5	5	13	9	3	1	3			42
1860	2	0	8	8	9	11	14	4	3		59
1870	7	1	1	2	1	10	28	13	2		65
1880	0	0	0	0	0	3	7	16	9	3	38

297

Loss: 6
(in private schools)

Table 14. The educational level of the cohort members

Cohort	No education	Elementary	Higher	Total
1830	46	0	0	46
1840	9	38	1	48
1850	3	39	1	43
1860	2	57	1	60
1870	7	58	2	67
1880	0	37	2	39
	67	239	7	303

Table 15. The distribution of the relative knowledge variable among the cohort members (see Appendix 2)

Co-hort	Relative knowledge value													Total
	4	5	6	7	8	9	10	11	12	13	14	15	16	
1840	29	12	1	5										47
1850	15	0	10	6	5	4	2							42
1860	4	0	1	22	9	10	5	0	3	2	1	0	2	59
1870	7	0	0	3	4	2	3	4	8	11	11	3	8	64
1880	0	0	2	0	1	1	0	1	9	7	10	1	6	38

250

Loss: 7 (higher educated)

B. Testing the models. Educational Achievement and Life-Path Development

The next step in the model testing was the comparison of the measures of real competence and life-path development. Here, however, we did not find the expected results. Diagram 31 illustrates the spatial spread of three age-cohorts and their migrational pattern from 10 to 40 years of age. The area inside the polygon formed by the spatial representations of life-paths greatly increases between the cohorts but it is important to note that the long-distance migrants were by no means an educational élite. Rather, the contrary was the case. Urban and interregional migration was dominated by the initially non-propertied groups; those who had acquired less knowledge at school according to the test of the first step of the model (see Tables 13–16). The non-propertied were also the most *frequent* migrants. The correlation between low socio-economic parental status and high spatial mobility was quite strong. As previously mentioned, Rundblad (1964) has shown

Table 16. Multiple regressions testing the first part of the proposed model

Age Cohort	Variance explained $100\,R^2$	Dependent variable	Independent variables	Direction of influence
1830	35.1	Own catechization	Socio-economy at ten	Positive
1840	24.1	register mark at	Mother's catechization mark	Positive
1850	9.1	age eleven	Father's catechization mark	Positive
1860	13.6		Number of siblings	Negative
1870	29.4			
1840	29.2	School mark for	Relative education time	Positive
1850	30.2	reading at eleven	Mother's catechization mark	Positive
1860	29.1		Father's catechization mark	Positive
1870	22.8		Socio-economy at ten	Positive
1880	26.6		Number of siblings	Negative
			Distance home-school	Negative
1840	25.1	Relative education	Socio-economy at ten	Positive
1850	19.9	time	Mother's catechization	Positive
1860	18.3		Father's catechization	Positive
1870	22.8		Number of siblings	Negative
1880	24.9		Distance home-school	Negative
1840	43.0	Relative knowledge	Relative education time	Positive
1850	48.9	at eleven	Mother's catechization mark	Positive
1860	36.2		Father's catechization mark	Positive
1870	49.9		Socio-economy at ten	Positive
1880	24.2		Number of siblings	Negative
			Distance home-school	Negative

that *geographical* mobility was high among the educational élite – a finding in complete contrast to ours. One explanation for this is the fact that, in agrarian society, almost all mobility between jobs was *spatial* mobility (migration). This was especially true for the landless, who lived in cottages or rooms belonging to the employer.

The relating of achieved socio-economic status to educational attainment yielded similar results. Diagram 32 describes the status development of individuals who belonged initially to the lowest stratum; as we can see there was little upward social mobility, regardless of educational attainment.

A regression test of the entire model showed that socio-economic status and spatial position at the age of 40 depended principally upon parental socio-economic status and, to a lesser extent, upon reading ability at school. This was the only comparable real competence measure for the different age-cohorts who had received formal education. *Direct resource* transfer was thus the main factor explaining socio-economic and spatial position achieved by the age of 40. Those people who were spatially stable consisted mainly of the initially landed, irrespective of whether they took over the parental position or not. A notable exception were the emigrants to the USA. These appear in the five later age-cohorts (1840–1880) – those with formal education – and especially in the

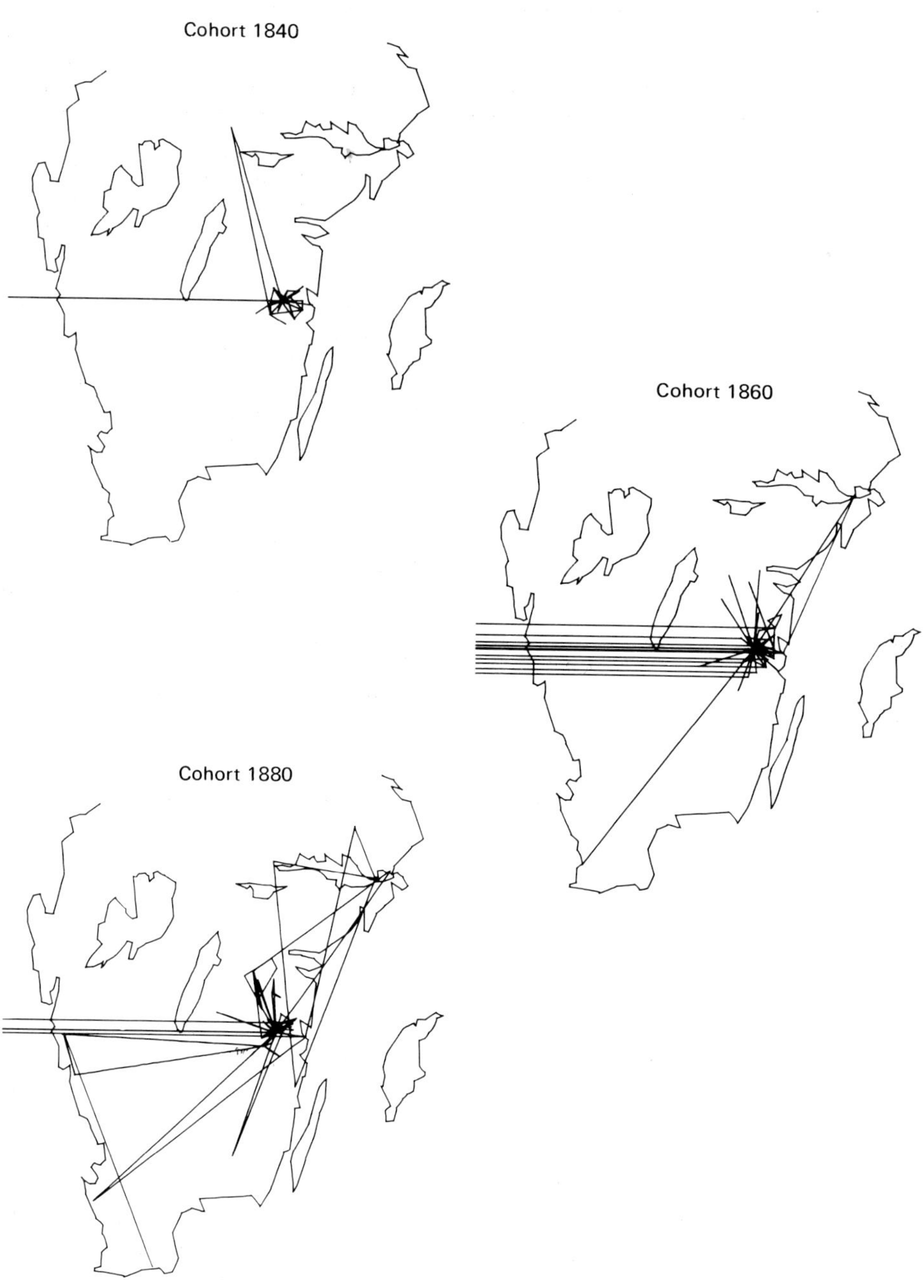

Diagram 31. Migration chains for age cohorts 1840, 1860 and 1880. Identical migrations are plotted upon eachother. Migrations within parishes are not plotted. Emigration to the U.S.A. is illustrated by horizontal lines pointing westward.

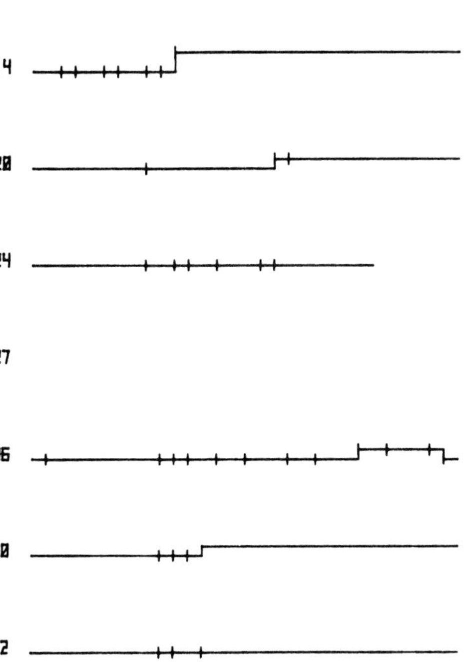

Diagram 32. Socioeconomic trajectories from cohort 1850 and with an initial status 6. Cross-strokes on the trajectory mark migrations.

Table 17. Urban migrants' social status at ten.
Permanently urban migrants

Socio-economy at ten	Cohort 1830	1840	1850	1960	1870	1880	Total
1	0	0	0	0	0	0	0
2	0	0	0	0	0	0	0
3	1	0	0	0	0	1	2
4	0	0	0	0	0	0	0
5	2	3	6	1	1	1	14
6	1	2	1	2	1	1	8
	4	5	7	3	2	3	24

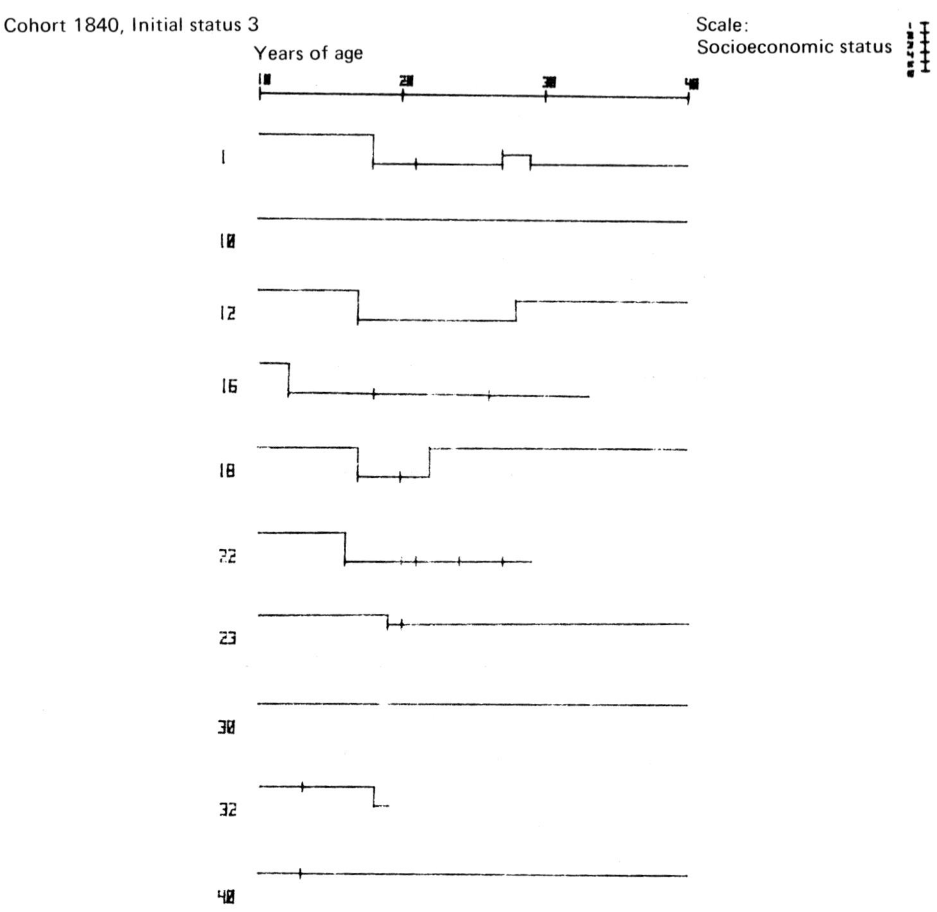

Diagram 33. Socioeconomic trajectories for a number of freeholders' children, initial group 3. Cross-strokes on the trajectory mark migrations.

Table 18.   Urban migrants' status at ten.
Migrants at some time living in an urban area

Socio-economy at ten	Cohort 1830	1840	1850	1860	1870	1880	Total
1	0	0	0	0	0	1	1
2	0	0	0	0	0	0	0
3	1	0	1	1	1	2	6
4	0	0	0	0	1	2	3
5	2	3	6	2	4	2	19
6	2	2	1	7	2	1	15
	5	5	8	10	8	8	44

cohorts of 1860 and 1870. With regard to real competence, there was an overrepresentation of people with high competence among the emigrants in the earlier age-cohorts (1840–1860) but an underrepresentation in the later cohorts. The emigrants were usually landless at the time of their emigration — in the 1840–1860 cohorts, for instance, a large number of proletarianized freeholders' children emigrated (an example is given in Diagram 33). The incidence of emigration can be generalized with diffusion curves (see Hägerstrand 1953) for groups with different social and educational backgrounds.

Let us now examine a few individual examples of life-paths:

1. **Carl Magnus Svensson (Diagram 34)** was born in Locknevi in 1840. His father was the tenant farmer of Hveneholm. Carl Magnus went to the Church school at Locknevi, which was quite close to his home, for 125 days out of 399 possible while he was of school age. His real competence was relatively high regardless of which measure we use; he was thus a typical representative of the initially landed stratum. In 1856, Carl Magnus moved to Korpebo croft as a farm-hand, in 1860 to the hamlet of Östankärr and in 1861 to the small estate of Skrikefall, still as a farm-hand. In 1864 he was married to a girl from distant Rystad in Östergötland and moved with his wife to Blackstad parish, adjacent to Locknevi. Three years later, the couple changed positions within Blackstad and moved to the Klefva estate where Carl Magnus still worked as a farm-hand. In 1868, the family moved on to a croft called Ärenäset and from there they emigrated to the United States in 1869. Carl Magnus can be seen as a typical example of the landed group which underwent proletarianization and, perhaps as a result, emigrated.

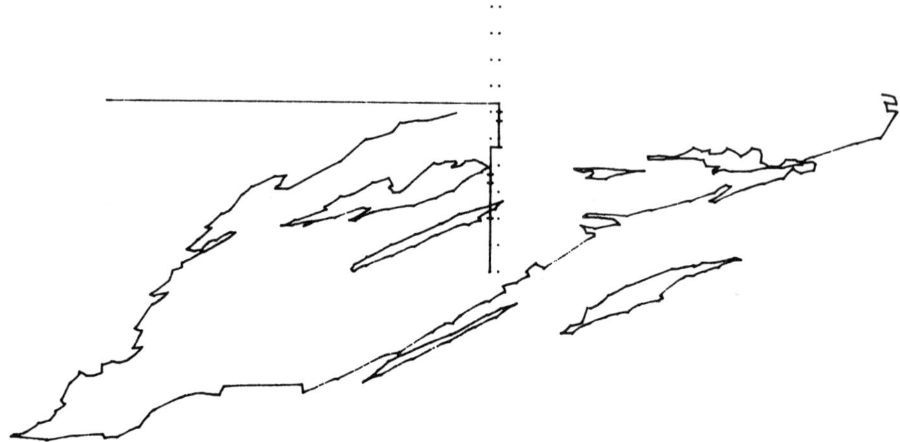

Diagram 34. Life path diagram for Carl Magnus Svensson, born in 1840, from 10 to 40 years of age. His dwelling on a parish level is illustrated by the dotted lines' cross sections with the map level. The vertical dimension expresses time. The temporal distance between every two dots is three years. Cross strokes on the trajectory expresses migrations within a parish.

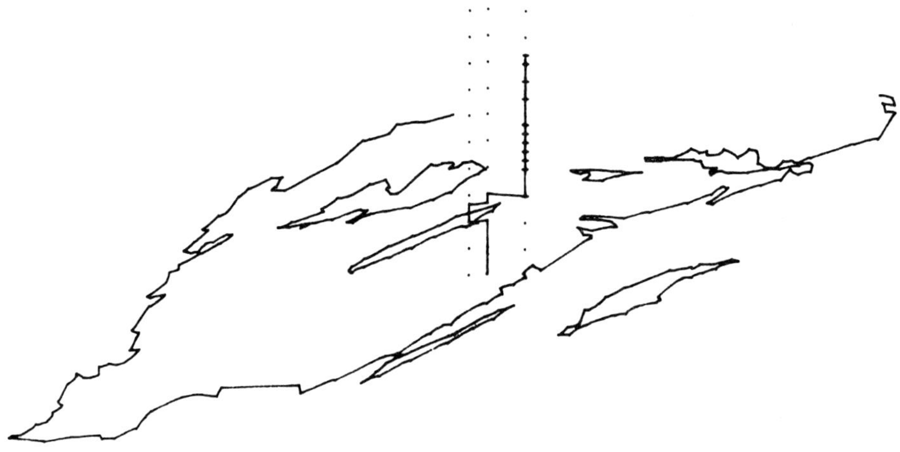

Diagram 35. Life path diagram for Sara Maria Adolfsdotter, born in 1840, from 10 to 35 years of age.

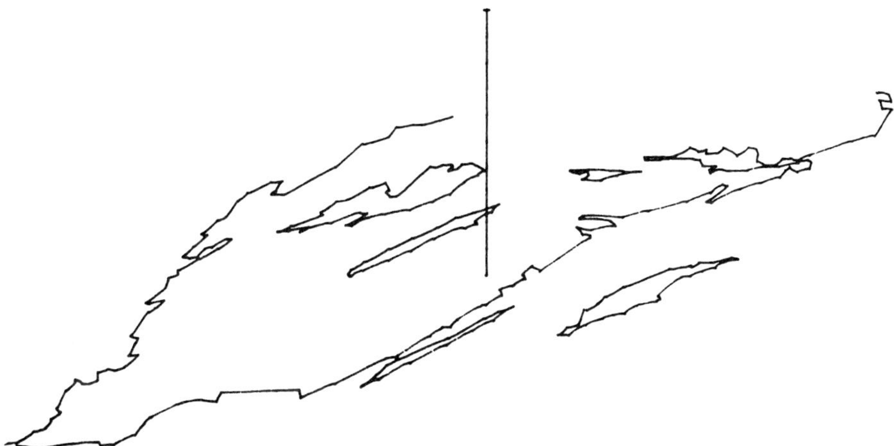

Diagram 36. Life path diagram for Ida Carolina Andersdotter, born in 1860, from 10 to 40 years of age.

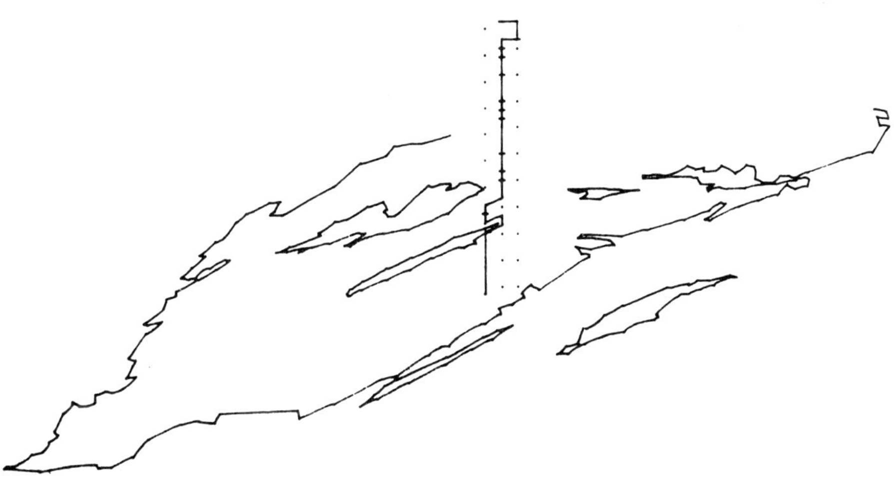

Diagram 37. Life path diagram for Gustaf Albert Gustafsson, born in 1860, from 10 to 40 years of age.

2. **Sara Maria Adolfsdotter** (Diagram 35) was born in Locknevi in 1840. Her father was a crofter on Äleviken croft, which belonged to the Toverum estate. In 1856, Sara Maria, after 50 days at school and with a low real competence moved to the neighbouring parish of Djursdala as a maid. In 1858, she moved on to the town of Västervik, still as a maid. As we can see in the life-path diagram, she was a frequent mover within Västervik, changing her spatial position almost every year. A decade later, she married a policeman but the couple continued to migrate frequently. By 1872, the husband had become a "former policeman" according to the parish registers, twice punished for illegal beer selling. In 1874 he received the title of "inn-keeper" in the Church examination register. Sara Maria died in 1875. She was quite typical of the rural-urban migrants in the population as she was landless and had a low real competence.

3. **Ida Carolina Andersdotter** (Diagram 36) was born in Locknevi in 1860. Her father was a small freeholder in the hamlet of Björkhult and thus belonged to the landed stratum. Consequently, Ida Carolina went to school for a moderate number of days, 130 out of the 400 offered in the Vrångfall school during her youth. Her real competence was high. In 1887 Ida Carolina moved to Elsebjörke farm where her husband became a freeholder, and she lived there for as long as she has been traced. She was a typical example of a non-proletarianized freeholder's child.

4. **Gustaf Albert Gustafsson** (Diagram 37) was born in Hycklinge parish, Östergötland (adjoining Locknevi) in 1860. At the time when Gustaf Albert was ten, his father was a crofter at "Pomern", which belonged to the Locknevi estate. Thus he was a member of the landless stratum. Gustaf Albert had a long way to go to school, almost seven kilometers, and his real competence was low as a result. He attended school for 158 out of a possible 440 days, which was rather little for his cohort, and his marks were also low. At the age of 17, Gustaf Albert moved to the neighbouring parish of Odensvi where he began work as a farm-hand at "Mogrind", a tenant farm belonging to the large estate of Odensviholm. There he remained for only one year, moving at the end of that time back to Locknevi where he found work on "Råshult" farm. In 1879 he moved to croft "Hvenefall" belonging to the Locknevi estate and from there in 1880 to Odensvi parish and "Brostugan" croft owned by Gällerstorp estate, still as a farm-hand. In 1882 he migrated to the Gällerstorp manor, in 1883 to Näringe and in 1885 to the "Mogrind" tenant farm which he had left seven years earlier. There he married and worked as a married farm-hand or "statare". During the 30 years that followed, Gustaf Albert migrated 15 times but never further than one parish, ending up in Odensvi from where he began his migrational career. He could be said to be typical of people who were landless, had low real competence and were highly migratory within a narrow area.

The hypotheses of Section VII:F have now been tested. Hypothesis 2A was refuted: higher real competence did not lead to an urban disposition of higher spatial mobility, although the high incidence of emigration might indicate a higher *potential* mobility, expressed as *real* mobility when proper chances became available. This supports hypothesis 2B. The third hypothesis — that higher educational achievement leads to a higher socio-economic level — received only weak support. The regression analysis revealed a weak relationship between educational achievement (measured as reading ability) and achieved socio-economic status. When relative knowledge was used as a measure (see Table 19) a similarly weak tendency was also discerned. Finally, the spatial search process may also have been affected by educational achievement, as the better-educated

Table 19. Relations between intergenerational social mobility and relative knowledge

| Cohort | Relative knowledge | | | |
	High value	Intermediate	Low value	Total
Positive (upwards) mobility				
1840	0	0	3	3
1850	0	2	3	5
1860	0	1	1	2
1870	2	6	1	9
1880	2	4	1	7
	4	13	9	26
Negative (downwards) mobility				
1840	1	2	11	14
1850	3	3	2	8
1860	0	2	4	6
1870	3	5	1	9
1880	2	4	2	8
	9	16	20	45

moved less frequently. This may well have been a product of direct resource transfer because the propertied and better-educated were generally able to take over established livelihood positions and so had less need to move.

It is now possible for us to describe the entire process of school establishment and its consequences. Educational background was an important influence upon individual school achievement — children from poor homes and from homes at a long distance from the school were apparently disfavoured. The pattern of spatial and social mobility was not markedly affected by the introduction of the elementary school as was the hope of Swedish liberals such as Rudenschöld (1846 and 1847). Within a restricted spatial domain, the landed were able to keep their positions from one generation to another through what we have called "direct resource transfer", while the landless were pushed out as competition for the available livelihood positions increased. In their futile search for an acceptable standard of living, the spatial representations of the life-paths of the landless are characterized by short moves and circular patterns. The effect of education on the pattern of mobility was small; we have shown that socio-economic status was influenced to some extent by real competence, but that the most dominant influence was inherited position. When children who were initially landed underwent proletarianization, they became more likely to emigrate or to take over a croft. The landless were thus pushed out of the local system — to the towns or out of the area. The resulting pattern is illustrated by the final positions of two of the age-cohorts studied (see Maps 30 and 31): the landless had moved far away and were often urban, while the landed had remained in the local area.

106

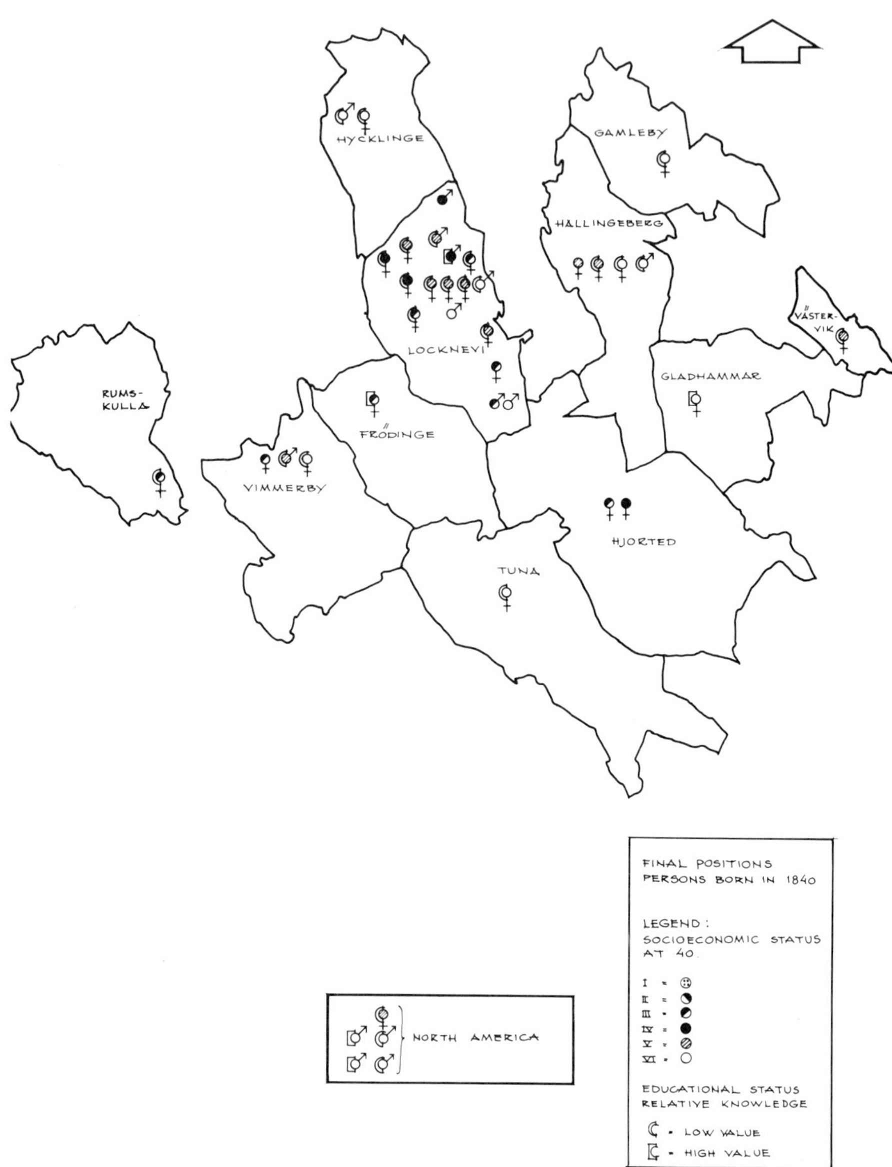

Map 30. Final positions. Persons born in 1840.

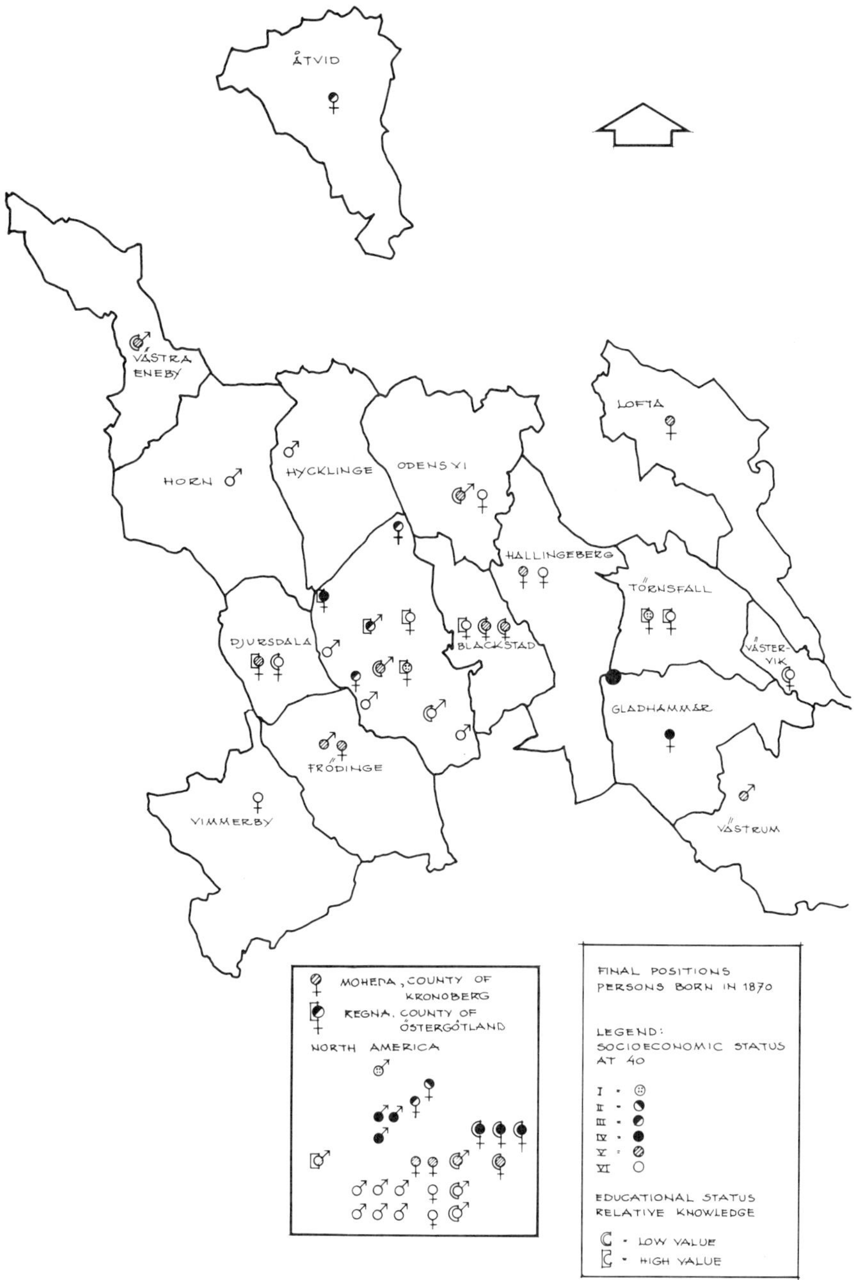

Map 31. Final positions. Persons born in 1870.

C. Testing the models. Formal competence.

This test was done using the test population born between 1928 and 1949 and living in Locknevi at the age of ten. The educational attainment of the population was at different levels — elementary school, secondary school, gymnasium etc. The population was divided into four age-groups in order to obtain a time-dimension, not only within life-paths but also between groups of life-path.

The persons were followed from the time at which they were 10 years of age until 1977. The life-paths were consequently of different length; some persons were 28 in 1977, others were 49. This had to be taken into account in the analysis as people of 28 cannot be expected to have achieved the same social and spatial stability as those of 49.

The rate of recruitment to higher education among this population has already been described in Chapter VI and there is no need to make further comment upon it. In order to test the second step of the model — the comparison of formal competence and life-path development — we must divide the individual life-paths into several dimensions. An example of this has already been given in the first model testing. The hypotheses proposed here are also formulated so as to make it possible to test one dimension at a time. In order to describe the effect of interrelationships between explanatory variables upon development, the entire model was tested by a series of step-wise multiple regressions after the initial hypothesis testing.

As before, the model testing was carried out using cross-sectional data from the individual life-stories. Of course, it would be more interesting to carry out a longitudinal testing in the proper sense but the methodological problems associated with this have not yet been completely overcome. Hence, it is possible to work either with individual examples or with the development of single variables over time, represented by trajectories, for example (see Hägerstrand 1962 and 1975).

Before we return to the testing of hypotheses, however, we should discuss the appearance of the life-paths for the different age-groups. For many of those growing up in Locknevi after 1930, there were few possibilities open in the home parish. Tiny fields and stony soil rendered farming unprofitable after the introduction of new techniques which were suitable only for well-shaped large fields. The youth of Locknevi were thus forced to take up occupations different from those of their parents if they were to maintain an acceptable standard of living. In general, that change consisted of movement towards towns, for most of the final spatial positions of the population studied here were located in urban areas. The longer an individual was traced, the greater was the probability that he or she would settle in an urban area. Those individuals traced up to the age of 49 should thus be located higher up the urban hierarchy than those followed only to the age of 28.

Yet there are several factors working against this. Firstly, urban growth has intensified over time; secondly, certain rural groups have changed their spatial behaviour patterns; and thirdly, according to our hypothesis, the level of formal competence in the population has risen over time thus further encouraging movement towards urban areas.

Of the 409 individuals studied, 102 were resident in rural areas in 1977, almost exactly 25 per cent. Of age-group 30 (those born between 1928 and 1934) 32 per cent were living in the countryside, while only 17 per cent of age-group 35 (those born between 1935 and 1939) remained in rural areas. Of the rural dwellers, only 58 our of the 102 were still living in Locknevi parish (14 per cent of the initial population).

The formal hypothesis testing was carried out by comparing pairs of variables. Hypothesis 2A proposed that higher formal competence leads to an urban disposition, due to the fact that livelihood positions with formal competence requirements are located mainly in urban areas. Table 20 shows the coefficients for the correlations between formal competence and urban hierarchy position; as we can see, there is a clear relationship. Hypothesis 2A is thus supported. Further proof can be found in Table 21.

Hypothesis 2B, that high formal competence yields high socio-economic status, was also supported by the testing. Tables 22–23 shows the coefficients for the correlations between occupational status and formal competence for when the subjects were 25 years in age and in 1977. There is a very strong association between the variables and, thus, no need for further verification. Finally, hypotheses 2C and 2D were tested by comparing the formal competence measure with, firstly, distance from Locknevi at the age of 25 and in 1977 and, secondly, the number of migrations made up to the age of 25 and up to 1977. One reservation should be noted: apartment changes inside a city might be under-represented in the kind of interview data used here because our migration measure normally registers only migration from one urban area to another. The relationships between the variables are illustrated in Tables 24–25. We can see that people with a high formal competence moved both earlier and further away from Locknevi but that, by 1977, the differences had diminshed. This can be interpreted as support for hypothesis 2C, i.e. those with low formal competence move to places close to the starting point. possibly step-by-step. However, the number of migrations made does not support this

Table 21. Absolute and percentage distribution of the studied 1928–49 population's educational level related to the urban hierarchy level of their respective dwellings in 1977

Education level	Urban hierarchy level											
	1	%	2	%	3	%	4	%	5	%	6	%
30												
1	26	35.1	14	18.9	28	37.8	2	2.7	1	1.4	3	4.1
2	4	26.7	2	13.3	6	40.8	0	0	0	0	3	20.0
3	0	0	0	0	2	33.3	3	50.0	0	0	1	16.7
	30	**31.6**	**16**	**16.8**	**36**	**37.9**	**5**	**5.3**	**1**	**1.1**	**7**	**7.4**
35												
1	17	22.4	23	30.3	24	31.6	6	7.9	4	5.3	2	2.6
2	0	0	4	26.7	7	46.7	0	0	0	0	4	26.7
3	1	9.1	2	18.2	3	27.3	1	9.1	0	0	4	36.4
4	0	0	0	0	1	50.0	1	50.0	0	0	0	0
5	0	0	0	0	0	0	0	0	0	0	1	100.0
	18	**17.1**	**29**	**27.6**	**35**	**34.3**	**8**	**7.6**	**4**	**3.8**	**11**	**10.5**
40												
1	27	36.5	11	14.9	30	40.5	4	5.4	0	0	2	2.6
2	2	11.8	4	23.5	7	41.2	0	0	0	0	4	23.5
3	0	0	1	11.1	6	66.7	1	11.1	0	0	1	11.3
4	0	0	0	0	2	100.0	0	0	0	0	0	0
	29	**28.4**	**16**	**15.7**	**45**	**44.1**	**5**	**4.9**	**0**	**0**	**7**	**6.9**
45												
1	19	35.8	7	13.2	20	37.7	2	3.8	2	3.8	3	5.7
2	4	11.8	4	11.8	23	67.6	3	8.8	0	0	0	0
3	1	14.3	0	0	2	28.6	3	42.9	0	0	1	14.3
4	1	7.7	1	7.7	6	46.7	4	30.8	0	0	1	7.7
	25	**23.4**	**12**	**11.2**	**51**	**47.7**	**12**	**11.2**	**2**	**1.9**	**5**	**4.7**

Table 20. Correlation (Pearson) between educational level and urban hierarchy level at 25 years, 40 years and in 1977

Age group	at 25 years	at 40 years	in 1977
30	<u>0.18</u>	0.38	0.32
35	0.50	0.34	0.30
40	0.33	—	0.38
45	<u>0.13</u>	—	0.30

Underlined values not significant on the 0.001 level.

Table 22. Correlation (Pearson) between household socio-economy level and educational level at 25 years of age and in 1977

Age group	at 25 years	in 1977
30	0.69	0.62
35	0.69	0.69
40	0.71	0.60
45	0.70	0.76

Table 23. Correlation (Pearson) between own socio-economy level and educational level at 25 years of age and in 1977

Age group	at 25 years	in 1977
30	0.81	0.73
35	0.83	0.79
40	0.79	0.70
45	0.77	0.83

Table 24. Correlation between educational level and dwelling distance from Locknevi at 25 years and in 1977

Age group	at 25 years	in 1977
30	0.23	0.11
35	0.44	0.26
40	0.46	0.41
45	0.41	0.28
Total population.	0.42	0.15

Table 25. Correlation between educational level and the number of accomplished migrations until 25 years and until 1977

Age group	until 25	1977
30	0.25	0.30
35	0.28	0.35
40	0.36	0.36
45	0.45	0.44
Total population.	0.33	0.35

argument, as we found significant positive correlations between formal competence and the number of geographical moves in all age-groups. As the interview data may not include all migrations, two alternative interpretations are possible. The first is that this correlation is incorrect and that migrations are not properly reflected by the measure. Nevertheless, it is not probable that the measure excludes so many moves that the correlation would be reversed. The second alternative is that the correlation is correct and hypothesis 2C is refuted..

We can conclude that high formal competence results in a high rate of spatial mobility. Spatial mobility also seems to increase over time generally. Although representatives of age-group 45 are in no case older than 32, the mean number of migrations is higher than that of age-group 30 whose youngest members are 43.

Hypothesis 2D, testing of sectoral barring and location in the urban hierarchy has already been partly supported by the testing of hypothesis 2A. We shall here test not only urban disposition, but also urban hierarchy disposition. The different patterns of location for persons with high and low formal competence are illustrated in Diagrams 38—39 and it is easy to see that the proposed hypothesis has been supported. Diagram 40 reproduces the final spatial positions in 1977 of one particular age-group and provides further support.

An analysis of all the variables in the model, using multiple regressions, showed that the *socio-economic level* achieved at the end of the life-paths was dependent mainly upon formal competence. Parental socio-economic status was significant as an explanatory variable to only a limited extent. The final *spatial distribution* of the population also depended upon formal competence as has been shown, although the specific spatial variables were not found to be highly significant in the multiple regression analyses. Another type of multivariate analysis such as path analysis may clarify the amount of interaction present.

It is interesting to note that the number of migrants to large urban areas did *not* rise between the age-groups, despite an increase in the number of people with higher education. The cause of this might be a concomitant increase in the levels of competence required for different kinds of livelihood positions.

As the number of highly competent people increases, employers can raise their competence demands (see Berg 1971). This is seen in the present-day large-scale youth unemployment which is affecting mainly those with elementary education, despite the fact that their real competence may be equal to that of people who has secondary level education in the 1950's. Diagram 41 illustrates this process schematically.

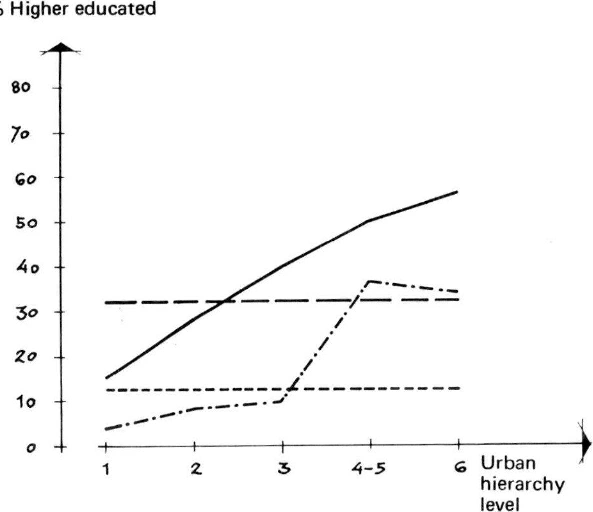

Diagram 38. Percentage higher educated of the total population at different urban hierarchy levels at the age of 25.

Legend:

─────────── = Percentage higher educated (above elementary education) at each urban hierarchy level.

─.─.─.─. = Percentage grammar school educated or above at each urban hierarchy level.

─ ─ ─ ─ ─ = Percentage higher educated or the total population.

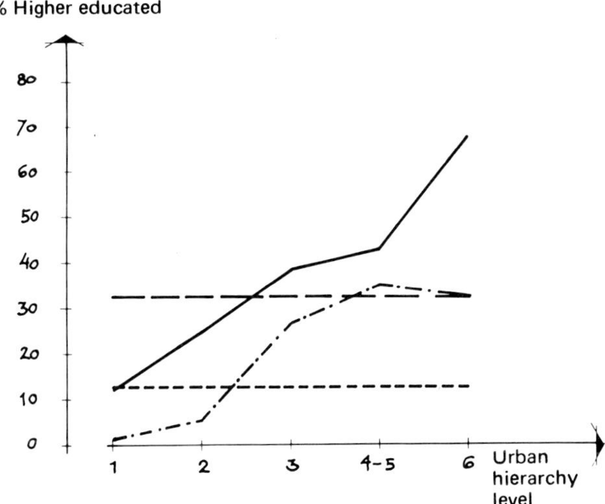

Diagram 39. Percentage higher educated of the total population at different urban hierarchy levels in 1977.

114

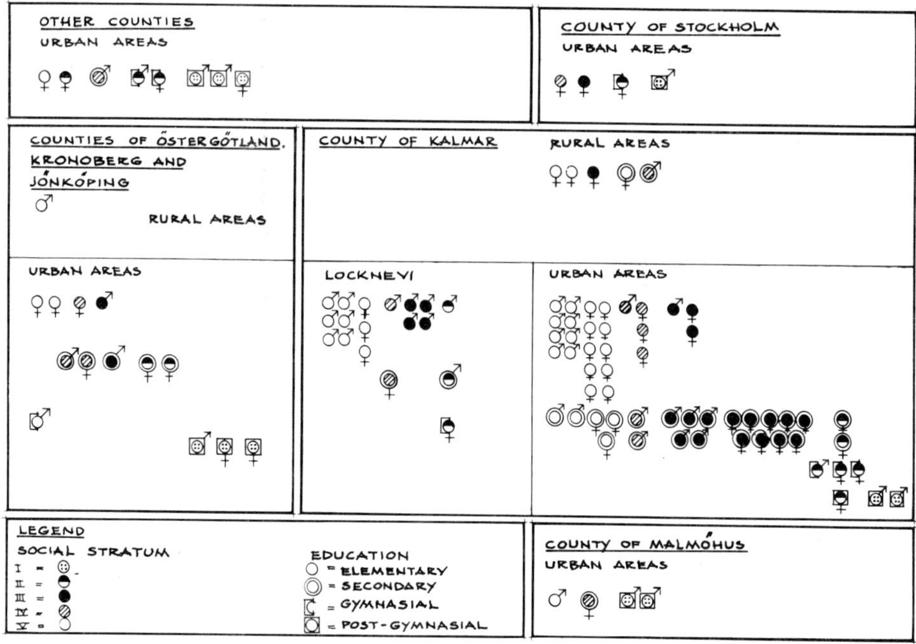

Diagram 40. The 1977 spatial positions of the 1945—49 age-group.

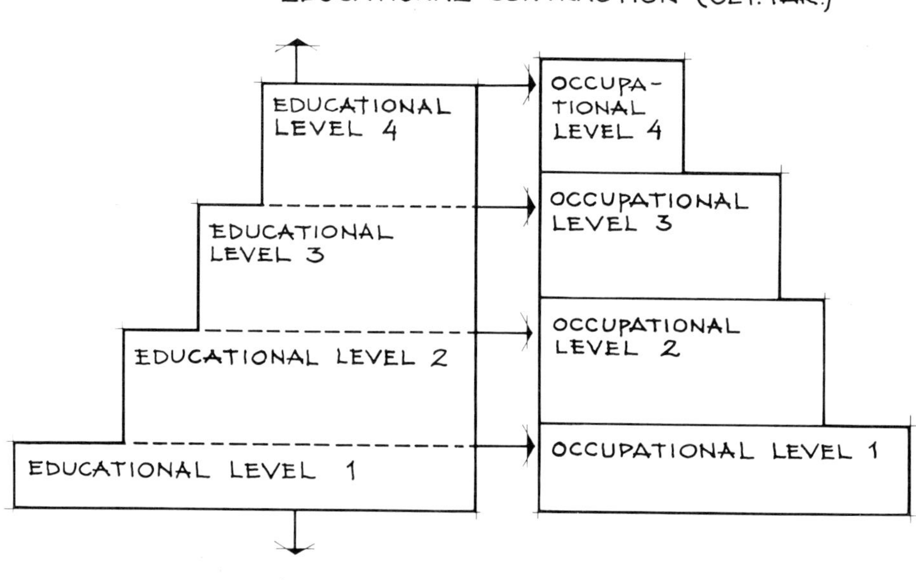

Diagram 41. Schematic description of formal competence demand in relation to educational supply.

D. Discussion

The results of the two model tests were quite different — in one case resource transfer was direct and connected spatially to the parental position; in the other there was both a direct and an indirect transfer in the form of resource conversion via education. In the former case, the theory was not verified in terms of the real competence dimension and life-path development; in the latter, the pattern of educational recruitment was not fully in accord with the predictions in Chapter VI.

We can thus conclude that in a society (or area) where resource transfer inside the propertied strata is mainly direct, the development of the knowledge domain through education will not have much influence on social and spatial achievement. During periods of change societies often come under pressure — one example is when many people are pushed out of their local system as the number of livelihood positions for some reason becomes insufficient. An enlarged knowledge domain may then help in evaluating different alternatives — for example, choosing North America rather than another region or urban area in the home country.

The rural population of the 1940's and 1950's was also exposed to stress. As the relative prices for agricultural products declined, rationalization became necessary and, where rationalization was not possible (as in many places in Locknevi), *production resources* lost their value. One reaction to this was the increase in educational status of the freeholders' children after 1955 and the consequent migration to urban areas. This migration was already apparent among those with elementary education in the 1935–39 and 1940–44 age-cohorts, and was also quite often the case after some years of working at home on the farm. As education had not prepared them for an urban future, the farmers' children in these age-groups often took up manual work. Through this "lack of phase accordance", a somewhat greater proportion of non-propertied children would have had access to higher education and, thereby, improved socio-economic status. The result was an increased social mobility.

If we relate the aims of education to the findings presented here, we may conclude that the liberals of the 1830's should have been disappointed, as the elementary school did not have any remarkable equalizing effects. From our perspective, this is not especially surprising because the society was hypothesized as having a system of direct resource transfer. Conservative powers such as the Church may possibly have had more reason for satisfaction. As we have seen, spatial and social adjustment was greater among people who had more elementary education.

In the industrial and post-industrial society of today where there is strong resource conversion via education (attained formal competence), education has not become "the Great Equalizer" as was once expected. But there is more chance for an initially non-propertied person to improve his socio-economic position today than a century ago; the social structure is less closed. This may be a result of the increasing importance of formal competence and the fact that fewer and fewer positions are inherited. In the transition from agrarian to industrial society, more opportunities for the spatially mobile, non-propertied strata become available, while spatially immobile, propertied strata may face temporary difficulties. When the new situation stabilizes, resource conversion increases and social mobility decreases. The process is discordant over time and space: marginal agrarian areas change first, central areas later.

Results of cross-sectional migration research which show that interregional migrants are more highly educated than, for example, the entire population of an area, appear where economic development is not uniform over space. Migration flows stimulated by circumstances in the homeregion tend to be more negatively selected. Examples of the latter situation can be found during the 19th century population "pressure" in Sweden; examples of the former in the depopulation of the countryside during the 20th century, as in Locknevi.

The role of education in life-path development differs, as has been shown here, according to the societal structure. Formal competence is probably the principal educational influence in societies in which livelihood positions demand formal qualifications; it is important in filling different positions and in transferring resources from parents to children. Real competence, in terms of the knowledge domain and evaluation capacity, is also of some importance in such societies; in 19th century society, however, it seems to have been of less importance. The knowledge domain is not entirely unimportant though, as the reatively high educational status of earlier emigrants to North America has shown.

Finally, we must consider the question proposed at the beginning of Chapter VII. The introduction of the elementary school may have changed the pattern of social and spatial structure to some extent but it was mainly a conservative factor. The expansion of voluntary education, on the other hand, directed the flow of out-migrants and exercised an influence upon people's migration decisions, as well as determining their future professions and, consequently, their future spatial positions.

REFERENCES

Anderson, A. (1962). "A Sceptical Note on Education and Mobility", in Halsey, A.H. (Ed.): *Education, Economy and Society*, New York.

Berg, I. (1971). *Education and Jobs: The Great Training Robbery*. Boston, Mass.

Bloom, B. 1964). *Stability and Change in Human Characteristics*. New York.

Boserup, E. (1965). *The Conditions of Agricultural Growth*. London.

Boudon, R. (1973) *Education, Opportunity and Social Inequality*. New York.

Bourdieu, P. (1976). "Kulturell Reproduktion och Social Reproduktion", in Lundberg-Selander-Öhlund (eds.): *Jämlikhetsmyt och klassherravälde*, Lund.

Boyle, J.F. (1977). "Educational Attainment, Occupational Achievement and Religion in Northern Ireland", *The Economic and Social Review, 8*

Caldwell, J.C. (1969) *African Rural-Urban Migration: The Movement to Ghanas Towns*. Canberra.

Carlsson, S. (1977) *Fröknar, mamseller, jungfrur och pigor*. Uppsala.

Dahllöf, U. (1971). *Svensk utbildningsplanering under 25 år*. Lund.

Dahn, P. (1936). *Studier rörande den studerande ungdomens geografiska och sociala härkomst*. Lund.

Ejdestam, J. (1969). *De fattigas Sverige*. Stockholm.

Ekbaeck, A. (1828). *Utförlig beskrifning öfwer Lochnevi lofl. församling*. Norrköping.

Ekstedt, E. (1976). *Utbildningsexpansion*. Uppsala.

Elgeskog, V. (1945). Svensk torpbebyggelse från 1500-talet till laga skifte. Lund.

Fogelvik, S., Gerger, T. and **Hoppe, G.** (1980). *Man Landscape and Society – An Information System*. Acta Universitatis Stockholmiensis: Stockholm Studies in Human Geography 2.

Fogelvik, S. and **Hoppe, G.** (1976). *Lägesbestämning av boställen: Locknevi församling 1846–50*. Kulturgeografiskt Seminarium 3/76, Stockholm.

Fägerlind, I. (1975). *Formal Education and Adult Earnings*. Stockholm.

Gerger, T. (1968). *Investigation into the Migrations of Manpower*. Stockholm.

Gerger, T. (1972). *Skolans geografiska utveckling i Sverige*. Stockholm.

Gerger, T. (1974). *Ett rumsligt förändringslopp; Den obligatoriska skolan i Sverige*. Kulturgeografiskt Seminarium 2/74, Stockholm.

Gerger, T. (1978). *Utbildning och samhälle*. Communications No. B 41 from Dept. of Human Geography, University of Stockholm.

Gesser, B. (1976). "Skolsystem och social skiktning". I Lundberg-Selander-Öhlund (eds.) *Jämlikhetsmyt och klassherravälde*. Lund.

Grigg, D. (1976). Population Pressure and Agricultural Change. *Progress in Geography 8*. London.

Habakkuk, H.J. (1971). *Population Growth and Economic Development Since 1750*. Leicester.

Hamilton, H.C. (1959). "Educational Selectivity of Net Migrants from the South", *Social Forces, 38*.

Hauser, R.M. and **Featherman, D.L.** (1977). The Process of Stratification. New York.

Helmfrid, S. (1961). The "Storskifte, Enskifte and Laga Skifte in Sweden", General Features. *Geografiska Annaler*.

Helmfrid, S. (1978). "Arealkonflikter vid tätortstillväxt – Problem för en samordnad regional och fysisk planering". *Att forma regional framtid*, Stockholm.

Herrick, B. (1965) *Urban Migration and Economic Development in Chile*. Cambridge, Mass.

Holm, E. and Häggström, N. (1972). *Regional rekrytering till universitet och högskolor under 1960-talet.* Umeå.

Hoppe, G. (1974). *Gymnasiernas geografiska utveckling.* Stockholm (Mimeo).

Hoppe, G. (1977). *Skolutbildning och individbanans utveckling.* Stockholm. Kulturgeografiskt Seminarium 5/77.

Hoppe, G. (1978a). *Formell kompetens och individbanans utveckling.* Stockholm. Kulturgeografiskt Seminarium 1/78.

Hoppe, G. (1978b). *Formal Education and Life-Path Development.* Stockholm. Kulturgeografiskt Seminarium 5/78.

Husen, T. with I. Fägerlind, I. Emanuelsson and R. Liljefors (1969). *Talent, Opportunity and Career.* Stockholm.

Hägerstrand, T. (1946). "Torp och backstugor i 1800-talets Asby". *Från Sommabygd till Vätterstrand III.* Linköping.

Hägerstrand, T. (1953, 1967). *Innovation Diffusion as a Spatial Process.* Lund.

Hägerstrand, T. (1957). "Migration and Area". In Hannerberg-Hägerstrand-Odeving: *Migration in Sweden.* Lund.

Hägerstrand, T. (1962). "Geographic Measuresments of Migration". In *Entretiens de Monaco en Sciences Humaines.*

Hägerstrand, T. (1975) "Survival and Arena". *The Monadnock. Clark University Geographical Society 49.* Worcester, Mass.

Jencks, C. (1972). *Inequality.* New York.

Johansson, E. (1972). *En studie med kvantitativa metoder av folkundervisningen i Bygdeå Socken 1845–1873.* Umeå.

Johansson, E. (1977). The History of Literacy in Sweden. *Umeå, Eduational Reports No 12.*

Lewan, N. (1975). "Urbanarealens expansion". Förändringar i SV. Skåne. SGÅ.

Lundsjö, O. (1975). *Fattigdomen på den svenska landsbygden under 1800-talet.* Stockholm.

Malthus, T.R. (1972). *An Essay on the Principle of Population.* 7th ed. London.

Neymark, E. (1961). *Selektiv rörlighet.* Stockholm.

Paulston, R. (1976). *Conflicting Theories of Social and Educational Change: A Typological Review.* Pittsburgh, Penn.

Pedersen, P.O. (1970). "Innovation Diffusion within and Between National Urban Systems". *Geographical analysis.*

Pedersen, P.O. (1971). "Innovation Diffusion in Urban Systems". In Hägerstrand-Kuklinski: *Information Systems for Regional Development.* Lund.

Pleijel, H. (1970). *Hustavlas Värld.* Stockholm.

Pålsson, E. (1958). *Gymnasiers rekrytering och lokalisering.* Lund.

Richardson, G. (1977). *Svensk Utbildningshistoria.* Lund.

Riddell, J.B. (1970). *The Spatial Dynamics of Modernization.* Evanston, Ill.

Rudenschöld, T. (1845). *Tankar om Ståndscirkulation.* Stockholm.

Rudenschöld, T. (1846). *Tankar om ståndscirkulationens verkställighet.* Stockholm.

Rundblad, B. (1964). *Arbetskraftens rörlighet.* Uppsala.

Törnqvist, G. (1967). *TV-ägandets utveckling i Sverige 1956–65.* Uppsala.

Winberg, C. (1975). *Folkökning och proletarisering.* Göteborg.

Åkerman, S. (1978). "A Population Before the Demographic Revolution". In Åkerman-Johansen-Gaunt (Eds.): *Change and Change. Studies in Scandinavian Historical Demography.* Odense.

APPENDIX 1 — The socioeconomic classification

The classification is performed from the various informations of professions that we have collected. For the 19th century population, six groups are utilized, four landed and two landless. For the twentieth century, two of the landed groups are amalgamated into one so a five-group classification is used. Wives are normally classified as their husbands, unless they are divorced or definitely to be considered a separate economic unit.

A.   The 19th century populations classification

1.   Estateowners
      Officers
      Major enterprisers
2.   Freeholders above 1/4 "mantal" farms (assessed value above 1/4 of this unit)
      Tenant farmers above 1/4 mantal
3.   Freeholders and tenant farmers between 1/12 and 1/4 mantal
      Master craftsmen
4.   Freeholders below 1/12 mantal, tenant farmers ditto, pensioned freeholders with guaranteed pension, craftsmen with their own minor business, rural merchants.
5.   Crofters, soldiers, craftsmen without their own business, gardener, farm foremen, industrial foremen.
6.   Cotters, hands, maids, destitutes, workers, sailors.

B.   The 20th century population classification

1.   Major estate owners, major enterprisers, academics with qualified tasks.
2.   Freeholders on the intermediate level, businessmen of smaller enterprises, schoolmasters, a.o.
3.   Smallholders, foremen, educated medical attendants, a.o.
4.   Crofters, minor office clerks, a.o.
5.   Blue collar workers, farmhands, etc.

See also Appendix 4.

APPENDIX 2 — The relative knowledge concept

This is simply a means to acquire one single measure from a number of school marks. The mark for reading is an exception though, as the 19th century pupils were supposed to be able to read when they started school as a result of the home education. The subjects compiled in this way were writing, mathematics, geography, history and natural science. The two last subjects were summed and divided by two as certain children has either subject in their examination. The marks were classified in the following way:

Mathematics $0 = 1$ $1\text{--}2 = 2$ $3\text{--}4 = 3$ $5\text{--}6 = 4$

so with the three subjects counted properly and the history/natural science divided by two, the maximum value of this variable was 16 and the minimum was 4. The level of relative knowledge goes up generally between 1840 and 1880 so that the mean goes from 4.6 in 1840 to 12.9 in 1880.

APPENDIX 3 — The operational urban hierarchy classification

1. Rural areas
2. Minor urban area   200–5000 inhabitants
3. Minor urban area   5001–25000 inhabitants
4. Major urban area   25001–75000 inhabitants
5. Major urban area   75001–150000 inhabitants
6. Major cities   above   150000 inhabitants

The number of inhabitants as well as the spatial delimitations of urban areas were taken from the 1960 cencus of Sweden.

APPENDIX 4 — The agrarian structure of Sweden

As the Swedish agrarians structure of the nineteenth century and before is quite different from its counterparts in, for example, England or France and as the terminology used is not directly translatable, there is a need for a brief explanatory note on the subject. As was noted in the text, there were three main types of land holdings: A) Land owned by freeholders and due for state taxation, B) Estates owned by the nobility and partly exempt from taxes, C) Land owned by the Church or the state. The social structure on each type of domain differed, as well as differing between domains of the same type. A generalized picture is given in Diagram 42.

A.   Domain A represents a freeholders hamlet.

Its inhabitants comprise three major categories, namely

1. *Freeholders* — independent farmers, obliged to pay taxes only to the state authorities and to keep a soldier (see below).
2. *Soldiers and crofters* — the crofters lived in crofts — small tenant farms which has no legal rights to the hamlet common but had a small area of arable and meadow. The crofts were usually located in the periphery of the hamlet domain and their arable plots were thus separate from those of the hamlet infields. The corfters (and their families) were obliged to work for the freeholder on whose land the croft was located for a certin number of days every year and sometimes also to pay rent.

    Soldiers normally had a somewhat better position than the corfters. Their crofts were located on the hamlet common land and formed part of their yearly ''salary''. The soldiers were not obliged to work for other farmers but as the crofts were usually to small to feed a family (below subsistence level), soldiers often undertook extra work as farm-hands or part-time craftsmen.
3. *Farm hands, lodgers and cottagers.*

B.   Domain B is an estate

Here we can distinguish four major categories or classes.

1. *The estate-owner and his family.*
2. *Tenant farmers, estate inspectors, etc.*

3. *Crofters* — the crofts were of generally the same type as those on the freeholders domains but — as Hägerstrand (1946) has shown — these crofters were obliged to do more work for the landowner. As estate owners were free from certain taxes, they did not need to keep soldiers which was a form of taxation.

4. *Farm-hands, lodgers, boarders, cottagers, etc.* Farm-hands were usually of two kinds — a) male or female unmarried hands living in, and b) married farmhands (''statdrängar'') living in separate buildings and whose wives also had certain obligations. These categories were at least partly paid in kind.

C. Domain C is an area owned by the Church of Sweden

Four strata are also distinguishable here.

1. *The vicar and his family*
2. *Tenant-farmers*, if any (sometimes the vicar functioned as an entrepreneur himself)
3. *Crofters*, generally of the same kind as under B
4. *Cottagers, boarders, lodgers and farmhands/maids.*

Generally speaking, stratum 4, cottagers and boarders, were kept under stricter control in domains B and C where *one* owner only was in command.

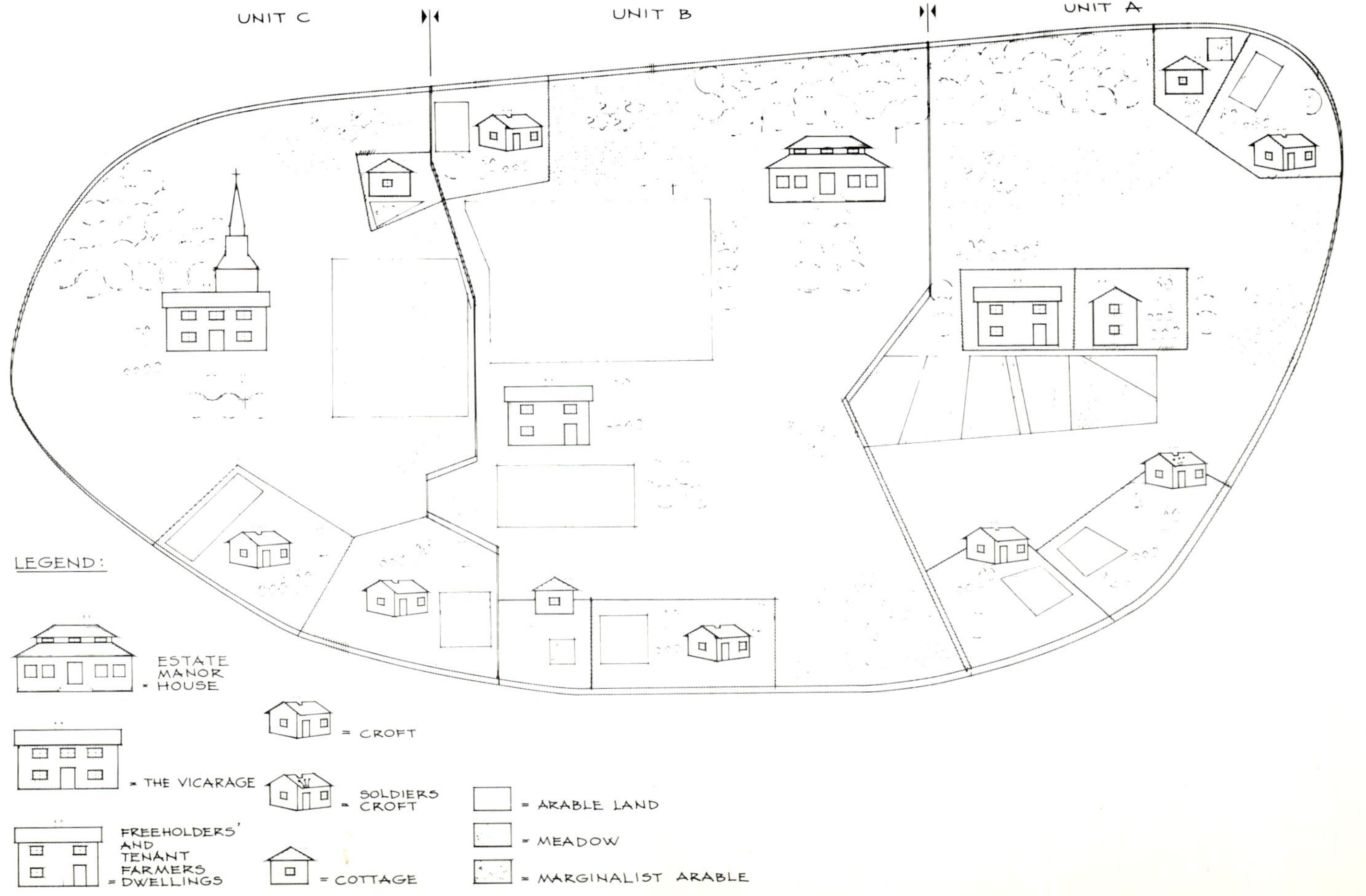

Diagram 42. A schematic outline of the Swedish agrarian structure of the 19th century. See Appendix 4 for further explanation.